To Catch A Bass

By Tim Coleman

MT PUBLICATIONS
MYSTIC, CONNECTICUT

Library of Congress Cataloging-in-Publication Data

Coleman, Tim, 1946-
    To catch a bass / by Tim Coleman.
                p.   cm.
            ISBN 0-929-775-04-X : $9.95
            1. Striped bass fishing – Northeastern States. I. Title.
    SH691.S7C64   1991
    799. 1'758–dc20

                                                    92-25639
                                                    CIP

Illustrations by Bob Jones

First printing – 1992
Second printing – 1994
Third printing – 1997

 **MT PUBLICATIONS**

No part of this book may be reproduced in any form without permission in writing from the publishers. Any questions, comments, etc. should be addressed to:

MT PUBLICATIONS
P. O. Box 293 • Four Avery Street
Mystic, CT 06355

About This Book

The striped bass has been part of my life since I caught a six pounder from the shores of Asbury Park, New Jersey, back in 1964. Whatever God you believe in has blessed me with the opportunity to travel and fish up and down the striper's shore ever since. My intense involvement with fishing led me in 1974 to go to work for The New England Fisherman, a weekly sportfishing publication. That extension of a desire to learn about the ocean and its inhabitants only heightened the possibilities of fishing with some of today's highliners.

From offshore of the broken down, busted up Humpback Jetty in Deal, New Jersey, to the swirling waters of the rip called the Elbow off Montauk to the sandy backwaters of Ipswich, Massachusetts, I've been fortunate enough to watch the best fool bass. This book is the result of those years.

This book assumes you have more than a passing interest in bass. It assumes you have a boat and mean to use it to the best of your talents. The tricks of the trade you are about to read belong to names too numerous to mention, some of which require anonymity to preserve a confidence. If you or someone you cherish catch your first legshaker from a tip herein, don't thank me, give a nod of the hat to people whose lives are built around catching stripers; people who generously took time to show a fellow fisherman what they knew.

Contents

1. Snagging Bunker 7

2. Gilnetting Bunker 13

3. Bait Tank System 19

4. Live Bait Primer 23

5. Casting Plugs 29

6. The Small Rod 37

7. Dropback Method 41

8. Basics of Wire 49

9. Tube and Worm 55

10. Trolling Worms 63

11. Bunker Spoon Primer 67

12. Taking Ranges 73

13. Loran Primer 77

14. Three-Waying Eels 83

15. Three-Waying Bunker 91

16. Three-Waying Bucktalls 97

17. Dunk a Chunk 103

18. Wire Line and Live Bait 109

19. Center Console Suggestions 115

20. Tin Boat Tips 121

21. Add-Ons and Additions 129

22. Bass Records 135

23. Casting Eels 137

24. Umbrella Rig Basics 147

25. Some Bass Rods 155

    About the Author 160

There's no more direct route to a trophy bass, week in, month out, than a bunker (pogy) sent to do your bidding in the local striper haunts.

CHAPTER 1

Snagging Bunker

It's a great day to be alive and out on the water. You've just bought a boat or you already have a craft and would now like to turn your sights to depositing a big striper in same. What's the best method to catch your first 40-pounder, especially if you wish to fish during the day? The answer is live bait and the most prevalent live bait, from New Jersey up through Maine, is the bunker or pogy, as they're called in New England. There's no more direct route to a trophy bass, week in, month out, than a wiggling bunker sent to do your bidding in the local striper haunts.

In the next few chapters we'll tell you how to catch your bait, keep it alive and, once on the fishing grounds, how to use it to your advantage. Most beginning bass anglers seek bunker in the early morning in a back bay, tidal river or estuary or, sometimes, in the open ocean. On a calm, still morning, bunker will flip around on top of the water. These tell-tale splashes give them away to fishermen looking to stock up their baitwells.

One of the most common methods to get bunker is with a weighted treble hook available in tackle shops all along the northeast shore. Using a seven foot or so spinning rod, with reel holding 15 or 20 pound line, cast the snatch hook into the area where bunkers are flipping. After allowing the hook to settle a bit, take the slack out of the line, then come back hard on the rod. The aim is to drive one of the points of the treble into the bunker. Once you have him snagged, you reel it in, then plop it in your bait tank.

To minimize damage to a bunker when snagging, it's best to bend down the barbs on the trebles.

Most bass anglers seek bunker (pogy) in the early morning in a back bay, tidal river, estuary or sometimes in the open ocean.

To minimize the damage to the bunker, it's best to bend the barbs on the trebles down. That way you'll be able to pull the hook out without unnecessarily ripping the bait, particularly if you've snagged it in the mid-section. Another trick is to use a four foot section of 50 to 60 pound mono leader between your fishing line and the snatch hook. After tying the snatch hook to one end of the leader, tie two 1/0 treble hooks with dropper loops at one-foot intervals up the leader from the treble. On the other end of the leader, tie a small, two-way swivel. This rig, cast into a flipping school of bunker, has three hooks working on your behalf instead of one, hence you increase your chances of a hit when you haul back on the rod. Like the weighted treble, the 1/0 trebles should be honed to fine points and the barbs bent down.

If you're fishing on the weekend, with anticipated heavy crowds as false dawn lights the sky, you can beat the rush by getting out a couple of hours earlier. If it's quiet that morning, you can hear the bunker flipping or see the swirls in the glow on the water from nearby dock lights. Two hours of this extra effort may require a larger cup of morning coffee, but it gets anglers on their way to the fishing spots while the majority of other boats are just looking for the first baits of the morning.

If you encounter a windy morning, all is not lost. You still have a chance to snag bait by running around the suspect area with you fishfinder running. Schools of bunker will show up as small, black blobs on a paper machine or different color splotches on a color recorder. When located this way, bunker can sometimes be snagged up and down, yo-yo style, as the boat drifts along.

One of the pleasant surprises to snagging is you just might catch a bass or blue right where you are getting your bait. Jumbo bass have been known to wander far up an estuary after frightened bunker. Ditto for jumbo blues which are also regularly caught right amongst sailboat moorings. Each year sees truly trophy choppers taken from the harbors along the western Connecticut and Long Island shores. The harbors offer sanctuary to bunkers trying to escape their doom by crowding in around mushroom anchors and drag chains. If you see bunker flying out of the water, jumping this way and that, it's very possible a blue will nail the bait before you get it back to the boat. If bass are around you might let the bunker go down under the schools, particularly if you're in

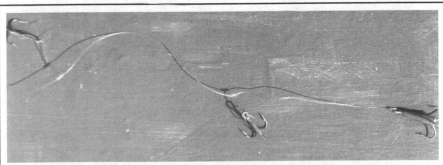

By using three trebles instead of one you increase your chances of snagging more bait.

It's possible to beat the weekend rush by getting up a couple hours earlier and snagging bait in the dark.

somewhat deeper water. Those same sailboat moorings that give up bluefish can also provide you with your 40 pounder. More than one Saturday bunker dunking trip ended successfully without ever leaving the harbor.

Note: if you're steaming along in your XYZ craft some morning, bound for the Guaranteed Grounds, keep an eye peeled for migrating bunker. More than one Jerseyite has stopped short of Monmouth Beach because he or she found bunker off the Convention Hall in Asbury Park. The flipping bunker are probably being corralled by gamefish. If you steam past them you run the risk of bypassing the 40-pounder. Several years back, a partner and I sat in a half acre of bunker off the Phillips Avenue jetty in Deal, N.J. Boat after boat passed up this massive invitation to catch a trophy. Finally, one boat stopped, not to fish, but to motor over to our small, red, tin boat to ask how fishing had been. Hastily hiding the broad tail of a 43-pounder under one seat, we answered the question with our best Christian smiles - in the negative.

Among the not-so-pleasant experiences of snagging bunker are mornings when the baitfish are few and far between. Those trips, by the way, are the ones when the bass usually bite the bottom of the boat. Getting bait on lean days via the snagging mode involves several hours to come up with a handful of livies. Those are times when a bluefish cuts your snagged bunker in two after you've spent the previous 59 minutes in fruitless yanking. Such calm mornings in August or nippy dawns in October might be the time to investigate other means of securing bait. That brings us to gill netting bunker, so please turn to Chapter Two.

Probably the best way to catch bait is with a 100-foot section of mono gillnet. Check local regulations, though, before purchasing one from a commercial fishermen's supply house.

CHAPTER 2

Gill Netting Bunker

Once you've got the knack of snagging bunker, it's time to move on to something better, something to replace the chore of endless snagging on mornings when each bunker is worth its weight in pictures of released 40-pounders. The answer to those days of small amounts of bait spread over a wide area is a 100-foot section of gill net. That amount of net, set out by one man in a small to moderate size bass boat, is capable of covering many times the water of the snagging rig. Two hours of using such a net can put a dozen baits in the tank when the same amount of bait would take until noon to obtain by snagging.

Pre-made bunker nets are sold at many commercial fishing supply houses up and down the striper's coast. At some locations they'll string a net for you to your specs. Some people might want slightly more or less net or perhaps there are local or state regulations governing the length of net allowed for bait-gathering purposes. On that note, we might also mention some areas restrict the use of gill nets inside a harbor or some states require the purchase of a bait license before you can go to work. And, expect to pay a fair price for a well-strung bait net.

Before we go further on gill nets, we might stop for a paragraph on cast

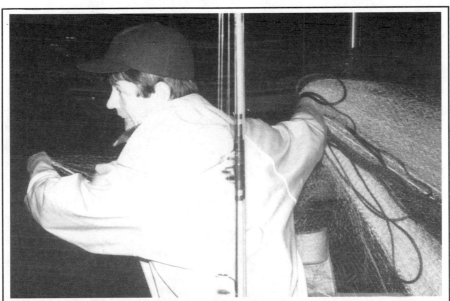

Cast nets can be used to get pogies (bunker) but they take practice to throw and the bait must be packed together for reasonable chances of success.

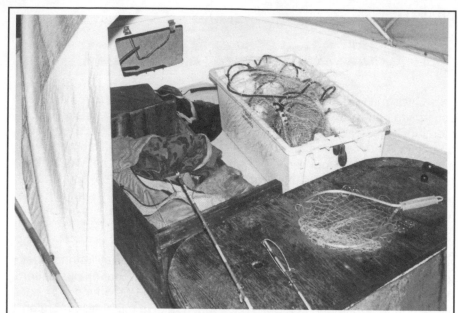

A bunker net can be stored in a plastic fish box. Make sure you keep it away from prolonged exposure to the sun.

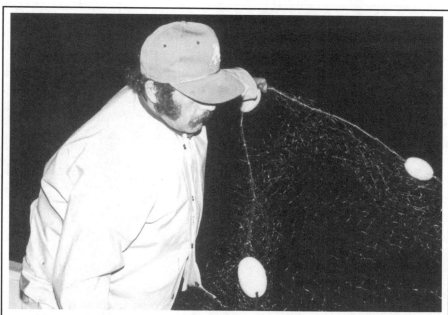

Always let the net out with the tide. It's not recommended to set your net against the current.

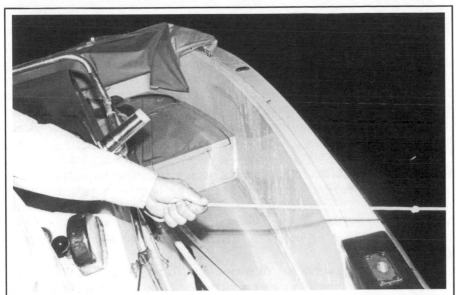

It's common practice to tie 15 to 20 feet of rope to the end of the cork line. After the net is set, the end of this rope can be tied off to your boat or held in your hand.

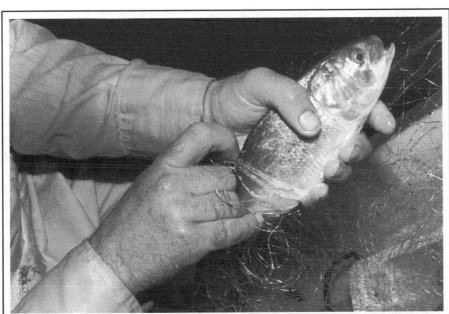

It's important to push the bunker through the net. Do not attempt to pull it back out.

nets. These are small, circular, mono nets cast out by a fisherman. The tossing of the net opens it up in circular fashion. Leadlines around the bottom cause it to drop on the water and sink rapidly, hopefully over a school of bait. A small rope tied to the thrower's wrist is pulled after the net sinks down. This drawstring closes up the net, trapping whatever bait it was cast over. Two drawbacks to the net are that it takes practice to learn to use it and the bunker must be reasonably packed in a spot when the leads hit the water or all you'll accomplish is to scatter bait not bunched together in the first place. For the most consistent results, in all kinds of bait conditions, try the gill net.

Usually a bunker net hangs down in the water about 8 to 10 feet. The top of the net is a length of rope onto which the netting is hung. Along that rope corks are spaced at regular intervals. These keep the net from sinking and also show you how it's laying if you choose to beat the crowd before dawn on Saturday. Along the bottom of the net is a series of small, lead weights which help the net hang straight down in the water. The mesh on the net should be three inches for adult bunker.

A good storage container for your new net is a plastic fish box available from the same commercial supply house that provided the net. Make sure you store the mono netting out of the sun, for prolonged exposure will cause it to become brittle and tear easily.

The next step in the process is to locate some bunker somewhere in your travels. It's not recommended to set your net in the middle of a circle of boats fishing the edges of a school of frantic pogies. Such a move might induce trauma that could require a physician's care.

Keep the net box close to the motor in the back of the boat. Once you've determined where some pogies are, run uptide or wind and begin letting out the net over the windward or uptide gunwale. If there's no wind or slack water, take the engine in and out of gear to provide movement to get the net out.

As you stream the net out of the side of the boat, make sure the cork and leads go out together or the net will tangle and not hang straight up and down. Some fishermen make it a point to tie a couple of 16-ounce sinkers to the far end of the lead line to serve as an anchor. Once all the net is out, it's common practice to tie 15 to 20 feet of rope to the end of the cork line. This can be held around your hand or tied off to the hand rail of a center console. Unless you're netting in a spot without current, it's important to set the net with, not against, the tide. Nets set against the tide will double back on one end, greatly reducing their effectiveness and have the owner reaching for the Excedrin. A trial run or two during the daylight is advisable before setting out at 2:30 a.m. to beat the weekend crowd.

Seeing how most cork floats on a bunker net are white, you can easily spot them trailing astern, even in the predawn darkness. Once you see one or more corks start to bob and wiggle, that's your signal to get ready to haul the net back aboard. The dipping floats mean bunker have unsuspectingly swum into the net and become gilled. If you leave them hanging there, so to speak, for too long, they'll drown since they will be unable to open and close their gills.

As you pull the net back in, make sure you pull both the cork and lead lines evenly, otherwise the net will not go out in a smooth motion. When you come to the first of your netted baits, grasp the netting, then push the bunker through; do not attempt to pull it back out. Unless you are looking for a year's supply of bunker, common sense dictates sparing use of the net when pogies are thick, otherwise you'll spend your day off picking bunker out of every hole in the net. On days when the baits are flipping all over, try to get off to the side of the main body so you get enough for a morning's fishing, not enough to fill up your neighbor's swimming pool.

Okay, now we have our baits but, before we call the taxidermist or get ready to collect the bet from your disbelieving brother-in-law, we must keep the bait alive on the way to the fishing grounds. That means we need a bait system in the family cruiser turned bass boat or your all-out fishing machine. Turn to Chapter Three to set up a bunker tank.

Components of a bait system are tank, pump, fastwater pickup, shutoff valve, overflow line and hoses. The pump is mounted on a stainless steel L-bracket below the waterline. The fastwater pickup is a piece of copper or PVC pipe with a small dog leg that sticks down under the boat. Forward motion of the boat forces water up the pipe, past a shutoff valve and into the tank. The pump, activated by a switch at the helm station, is used when the boat is drifting; the pickup while the boat is underway. These two components insure that fresh, circulating water is going into the tank all day, the key to healthy live bait.

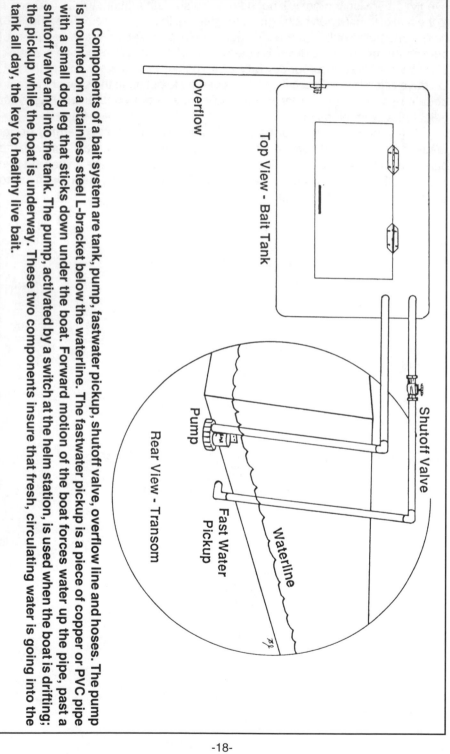

Top View - Bait Tank

Overflow

Shutoff Valve

Pump

Fast Water Pickup

Waterline

Rear View - Transom

CHAPTER 3

Bait Tank System

To get your bait from tidal bay or river to the fishing grounds, you'll need some type of container to keep them in. Some folks will get by with a plastic garbage pail with buckets of sea water poured in for aeration. Others, though, want something a bit more effective, a bit more professional.

Several companies make fiberglass or polyethylene live tanks for today's increasing population of striper fishermen. These companies offer plain tanks or some with hose fittings already attached. All the containers have removable or hinged tops to provide access to your baits. Two companies that make bait tanks are Marine Bait Saver, 315 Jefferson Blvd., Warwick, RI 02888 and Caddy Company, 57 Bayonne Avenue, Central Islip, NY 11722.

Before we begin to outfit your tank with plumbing fixtures, a word about

Some trial and error may be necessary to determine the best place in your boat for your tank. Here a 52-gallon tank has been placed between the console and casting platform in a vintage 19' Aquasport. Curved teak blocks on both sides of the tank keep it in place while underway.

placement in your boat. Water weighs eight pounds to the gallon, so a 30-gallon tank, when full, adds 240 pounds to your rig. I used to have a vintage, center console, 19-foot Aquasport into which I put a 52-gallon tank. The added weight behind the console made for a poor ride on a lumpy day. The extra rpms needed to keep the boat up on plane produced a crash-banger of a trip. However, with the same weight between the console and casting platform, the boat rode well indeed. On the converse side, a friend who is a master bass fisherman, steadfastly maintained the place for his bait tank in his 20-foot center console Sea Craft was behind the steering wheel. Some trial and error may be in order for your rig.

The larger the tank, the more bait it will hold. My 52-gallon model could easily handle 25 adult bunker all of the fishing day. A tank with half that capacity would reduce the amount of bait proportionately. Coupled with the size of the tank is the amount of water a small bilge pump, a vital ingredient in our plumbing system, can pump into the tank. A pump pushing 500 gallons per hour will suffice on average. For the angler who wants a bit more, I'd move up to one that handles in the neighborhood of 1,300 gallons per hour. The extra money for such a pump might be worth it on a day when you don't

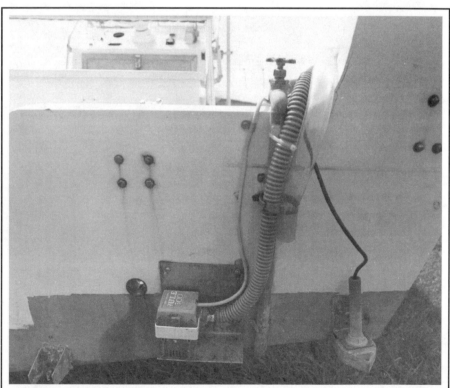

Stern view shows pump mounted below the waterline on a stainless steel bracket. To the right of it is the fastwater pickup/shutoff valve and the clear hose to the far right is the overflow line.

Top view of hoses and pipe for pickup, pump and overflow.

find the fish until just before closing time. Then, those four or five baits kept lively by the extra volume of water might pay off in your first 50 pounder.

After you've determined where your tank is to go, you must then make sure it doesn't move around while you're moving from one hotspot to another.

Fisheye view of the fastwater pickup below the hull.

The boatyard that did the work on my Aquasport fashioned pieces of teak to the exact outside curvature of the tank. The pieces were screwed to the deck, then the tank put in place.

Next step was to cut a hole in one side for a drain plug. Make sure the plug is up above whatever means were used to keep the tank in place. The plug is needed to get the water out of the tank at the end of another successful day at bass hunting.

The plumbing system is comprised of some inch and inch-and-a-half hose, small bilge pump, stainless steel L bracket and shutoff valve. Once I had all the components, the work was done by a competent person, not a first-time do-it-yourselfer. It was a system that lasted three years, trouble free, until the boat was sold.

The first step is to mount the pump on the L bracket and then mount both of them on the transom, below the water line. Usually pumps have a wire that runs from them to a switch which turns the pump off and on. I had the wiring run up to a switch installed right on the console dash with my others. It was only a simple matter to reach out and start the operation.

A section of the one-inch hose connects the pump to a fitting installed in either the side or top of the tank. Once the hose is connected, the water is sucked into the pump, then pumped up into the tank. In the case of tanks mounted in front of a center console, it might be a good idea to run the hosing up under the gunwale to keep it out of the way.

The next step is to mount a fast-water pickup on the transom next to the pump. The pickup is a length of copper or PVC pipe that reaches down under the hull thanks to a 45 degree bend in its end. The forward motion of the boat forces water through the pickup, past a shutoff valve, into another length of hose, up past another fitting, into the tank. The shutoff valve is the type used on your garden hose. If you don't want water going into the tank, all you have to do is close the valve. We might mention some folks install a Y valve and switch it from pickup to pump, and vice versa, depending on their fishing mode. The Y valve requires only one section of hose going into the tank - and the boat.

Once the tank is full, you'll need an overflow fitting put near the top of the tank, off to one side. It's best to use slightly larger hose for the overflow; in this case that means inch-and-a-half instead of one inch used for the first two steps in your bait tank plumbing. Once the water in the tank reaches a certain level, the water exits through the hose and out the back of the boat, With this system it's possible to have fresh water going into your baits whether the boat is moving or at rest. If the boat is drifting along, all you need do is turn on the pump. If the boat is moving, open the shutoff valve. In both cases, the baits in your tank receive a continual dose of fresh, life-preserving water.

Note: all the plumbing on the transom can be secured with stainless clamps to make a nice, shipshape profile.

CHAPTER 4

Live Bait Primer

The preceding chapters took us through catching bait and keeping it alive. Now it's time to go fishing.

With a tank of frisky bunker, you're now in an area where bass are biting the prop off the outboard. Okay, okay, so perhaps there were a few bass rumored taken in the spot last week. In any case, the sun is just coming up (the best time for bass), you've got a fresh bait out of the tank, what now?

The best tackle to use livelining for bass is a conventional rod of six to seven feet with action comparable to a 30-pound class trolling blank. This type rod has action to provide sport with a 20-pounder yet has enough muscle when your 45-pounder takes hold. There are many fine factory rods on the market which will fill the liveline bill nicely. Your local tackle dealer can help you here or you might consider a custom-made rod. Reels that compliment such a rod are the Penn Jigmaster or 112H, Diawa 50H or 300H, Garcia 7000 or 9000 and the Shimano TLD 10 or 15. Choose a good quality line like Ande, Stren or Berkley and fill the reel with 20- to 40-pound mono. If you're new to the game, go with 40, but the lighter line will bring more strikes.

Some anglers prefer a short section of 50- to 60-pound mono as a leader between running line and the bait. Others just tie a hook on their line and begin fishing, I'd recommend some Mustad trebles in 1/0 or 2/0 sizes to start with. Tie the hook on your line, then insert the hook in the nostril opening on top of the bunker's mouth. Don't insert the hook point too deep or you'll kill the bait. Just run the hook through one opening then out the other. Hooked this way, bunker

Insert the hook in the nostril openings on top of the bunker's mouth.

Take your reel out of gear and let the bait swim out into the payoff zone. Some trips a bass will nail the bunker 100 feet from the transom.

When a large bass rises to take your bait, she'll likely make a large swirl on top.

Let the fish run with the bait for a count of four, then set the hook.

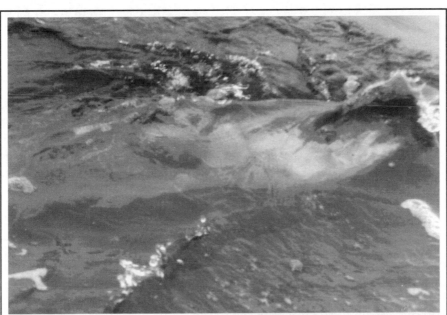

A large bass will usually make one long, speedy run after she's hooked. Once you turn her, a steady pump and reel will bring her to the boat.

will swim in good fashion for a long time - or until a bass interrupts his freestyling.

Bring your boat to bear on a point of land, jetty front, rocky beach, hole in an offshore bar or wherever your common sense says a bass is hiding. Get in close enough to do some good, but watch the oncoming seas. Next step is to put the bunker in the water, take the reel out of gear and let the bait swim out into the payoff zone. Some trips, a bass will nail it 100 feet from the transom. More bass over 40 pounds have been fooled that way than a lot of grizzled old-timers would care to admit. Yes, sometimes it's that easy.

As the bunker is swimming around, keep your reel in free spool with your thumb on the spool. A bass eying the bait will usually give away its presence by making the bunker nervous. Where your bait was swimming steadily five seconds before, now he starts to buck and swim this way and that. The jerkier its movements, the closer you are to getting your first strike of the day.

When that 30-pounder rises to grab the bait, she (most large bass are female) will make a large swirl on top. When you feel the fish has the bait in its mouth, let her swim off a count of four, then flip the reel in gear and set the hook. A 40-pounder will burn off line in her first rush. Just hang on until she stops, then apply steady pressure. If you've hooked a real titan, the fish might stop, shake her head, then steam off more. If that happens, you've hit a fish on steroids or have the hook into something 50-plus. Once you've turned the fish, slowly pump the rod and reel it to the boat. Don't allow any slack.

If the fish is going home with you, strike it with a gaff or use a large net in states that don't allow the use of a gaff. If you're going to release the bass just unhook the small treble or clip the line if the fish is hooked down its mouth. The hook will rust away in time.

Some days the bass will come up and swirl but will not grab hold. Such antics from a 40-pounder are not recommended for those with pacemakers. If

It's possible to troll a live bunker just like a plug or other lure.

Some days, it's very easy to catch huge bass with live bait. But, on other tides, you may have to reach into your bag of tricks.

you encounter one or more fish like that, you have some options. One is to take a small scissors and clip the bottom part of the tail fin, this will slow down the prize enough for a fat, lazy striper to get it. If that doesn't work, what you might do is slowly troll your live bait. Yes, that's right, troll it like you would a lure. Let out 150 to 200 feet of line, then motor back and forth across your striper hotspot. This is the reason for hooking the bait in the nose. A bait hooked in front of the dorsal fin would not be able to be trolled along in natural fashion. Don't ask why, but bass will grab a bait being trolled when they only play with one being livelined.

The best speed for trolling live bait is just above stop. With a small outboard that's no problem. Anglers with big block engines can take the boat in and out of gear or perhaps toss a five-gallon basket, attached to the transom with a rope, over the side. This will slow the forward motion to the speed necessary.

As you troll away, keep the reel in free spool with your thumb on the spool. If you're running the boat, it obviously means you'll have to handle the skippering chores and the rod at the same time. Once again the bunker will get nervous as doom approaches from below. When this happens, some anglers take the boat out of gear to await the initial explosion that may or may not happen. Sometimes you'll see the dorsal fin of the bass cut the water in hot pursuit of a bait fleeing for its life. This, too, is not recommended for those with coronary problems.

When the bass has your bait, let it run with it. It doesn't take long for a 30-pounder to inhale an adult bunker. Come back on the rod, then hang on as the bass runs away from the source of its panic. A slow pump-and-reel will bring her to you unless she's fouled the line in weeds or rocks on the bottom. Foul areas often call for 40-pound line. If your bass holes are all sand, go with 20-pound.

On Wednesday, you might find the fish hit the bait as you troll into the tide, while Thursday they prefer it the opposite way. Then there's the weekend when they hit it coming and going. Those are the days you remember, but don't exceed the legal limit; the more you release, the more will be around next season.

Here's one final tip to fool the playful stripers. Take a fresh bait then, with your rod, cast it high in the air with a trajectory that will bring it down near home plate. You want the bait to hit the water with as big a splat as you can muster. Casting a pound-and-a-half bunker takes practice but it pays dividends on the tough days. Don't ask why it works, but some bass may hit that bait after ignoring ones livelined or trolled atop their doorsteps. Then again, bass may not have read this book, choosing instead to ignore all offerings until the next tide.

CHAPTER 5

Casting Plugs

Some of the brightest memories of my bassfishing career were those spent during first light, in the back of various boats, tossing large surface swimmers into the white water around rocky points or jetty fronts. Nothing gets the day in perspective like a 30-pounder boiling up to eat that piece of wood.

The plugs I liked the best were these six- and eight-inch models made by the late, great plugmaker, Danny Pichney. Danny fashioned 2-1/4 and 3-1/2 ounce enticers that swam seductively on the surface, leaving a V-shaped wake in their path. Bass and bluefish, out prowling in the early light of dawn, would often find out the error of their ways by mistaking one of Danny's creations for something alive.

Luckily, Stan Gibbs Lures has come to the rescue of fishermen who cherish the art of casting wooden plugs into the breakers. Today, they market Danny surface swimmers, keeping a tradition alive for the thousands of fledgling bass addicts now in the making.

Sturdy tackle is needed to cast such large lures into the front of the Humpback Jetty in Deal, New Jersey; the rocks in Turtle Cove, Montauk, New York; Hen and Chickens Reef, Westport, Massachusetts, and the rocky areas adjacent to the mouth of the Saco River, Saco, Maine. A spinning rod in the

The late Danny Pichney and one of his many great creations,   the Danny Surface Swimmer, a bass fooler par excellence.

Don't be surprised when a hungry bluefish grabs the swimmer meant for bass.

Nothing gets the day in perspective like a 30-pounder boiling up to eat that piece of wood.

seven-foot range should suit most anglers. The heavier models of the Penn Slammer Series fill the bill nicely or, again, your local tackle dealer can help you out with other factory selections or perhaps a custom stick. The ol' standby of the Penn 750SS Spinfisher will compliment a Danny plug rod when wound with quality 20-pound mono. Fishermen who favor conventional tackle will like the Garcia 7000 with 20- to 30-pound line. The same seven-footish blank, but this time with conventional guides, will nicely handle the large Dannies as well as do double duty as a lighter version of a live bait rod.

The standard rigging for plug casting is about a 30-inch piece of 50- to 60-pound mono for leader. A small, two-way swivel goes on one end of the leader, a rounded snap on the other. The rounded snap will enhance the side-to-side waddle of these lures rather than constricting it as would be the case with a snap with V-shaped end. Those tend to reduce the action since the front loop of the lure will bind up in the V. The rounded-end snap reduces the binding to almost naught, thus more lifelike action.

Favorite places to cast the lures are the fronts of jetties, rocky points with boulders awash or wave-washed reefs that pull to within 20 feet of the surface. Bring your boat safely within range of these spots just as the sun brings the first light of the day. If possible, put the lure right in the suds, then start a slow, steady retrieve. Be alert on your first cast for, if there are bass underfoot, they'll take hold quickly.

If you get a swirl behind the plug, slip it right back to the same spot the second cast. If you get another look but no sale, try hauling back on the rod just

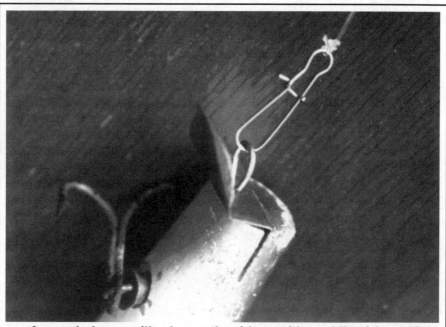

A rounded snap will enhance the side-to-side waddle of the surface swimmers.

like you would with a popper. This will cause the lure to push forward in the water, throwing spray as it goes. The splashing sometimes makes up the mind of a hitherto unconvinced striper.

Another addition to your bag of tricks is to tie saddle hackles on a single hook on the back of the lure. When the lure waddles along, the hackles sway this way and that, beckoning a bass to take a further look.

As the sun rises, the inshore action might drop away to nil unless, of course, you hit that magic, overcast day in the spring or, perhaps, strike a mother lode of bait in the fall. At 9 a.m. on the average day, your casting needn't be done. Head out to an offshore reef, should your area possess such. Cast the Dannies around the knob on the top of same, using the cast and splash method of retrieve. Slammer blues will not like that big so-and-so baitfish swimming over their heads. They will come out of 20 feet of water to hit the intruder; sometimes out of cussedness as much as hunger. Pick a day after a storm, when fish have been off the feed bag because of dirty water, and you can have a day deserving of a photo in the scrapbook or mention in the fishing column of the local press, in just such a spot.

Come sundown on an average day, you'll want to be back at your inshore haunts looking for more bass. The last hour, after the sun has set but before it's fully dark, is the time you can really fool sharp-eyed fish that may have only looked and swirled before. The best sea condition for Danny fishing is a light to moderate surf. That big, plodding lure stands out like a neon sign as it swims along, an easy mouthful for a jumbo bass so inclined.

For daytime fishing, I like an all-white plug or one with white belly and blue top. If you like to stick around your bass haunts after dark, an all-black

Another addition to your bag of tricks is to tie saddle hackles on a single hook on the back of the lure. When the plug waddles along, the hackles sway this way and that, beckoning a bass to take a further look.

Danny will fool 'em but, remember to watch for rocks eating the lower unit or the push of an incoming sea. On a full moon night, try an all-white Danny.

Dannies will obviously work once the sun is gone for the day. Many years ago, when the elders complained about rock and roll instead of heavy metal, I showed a surface swimmer to a companion of mine in a small tin boat bobbing off the front of McClintock Avenue Jetty in Ocean Grove, New Jersey. My partner wouldn't believe July bass would come to grab a plug right off the surface. Three chunky 10-pounders later he was convinced. The same slow, steady retrieve you used to fool your 20-pounder last Thursday morning will work on a Friday night tide. That is, of course, if your boss has forgiven you for being late for work on Thursday.

I've never caught a 50-pounder with a Danny though others have. They regularly fool enough fish in the 15- to 30-pound range to warrant an entire chapter in this book. Since you already have your "bait" on board, it's possible

The best sea conditions for Danny fishing is a light to moderate surf. That big, plodding lure stands out like a neon sign, an easy mouthful for a jumbo bass so inclined.

to go fishing a couple hours without the need to get bait. However, while they are effective, they are not a substitute for a live bunker. Dannies, though, will work on some mornings late in the season when you stop off on a jetty front for a few casts before heading out to spend the rest of the day chasing inshore cod or perhaps blackfish. Dannies can go with you if you take your boat on a fishing vacation to the fabled island of Cuttyhunk or further up into the bass-rich water of the far reaches of Maine. Dannies are also at the ready if you find blues or large bass chasing bunker some night in a tidal river or estuary, a short cast from your marina. To borrow a line from an ad, I wouldn't leave home without them.

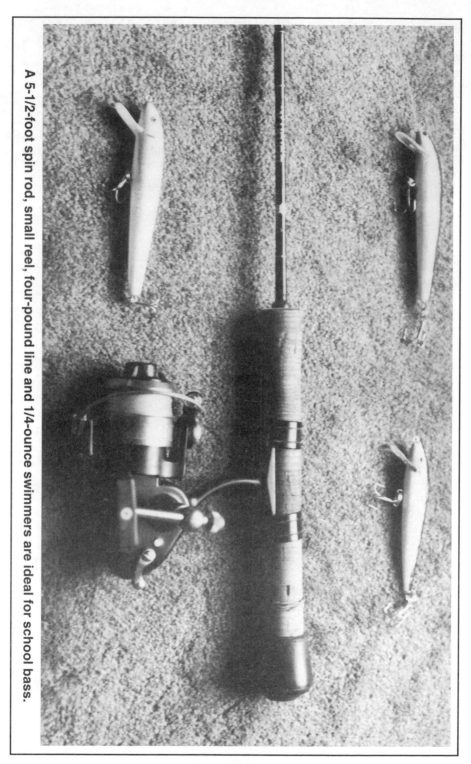

A 5-1/2-foot spin rod, small reel, four-pound line and 1/4-ounce swimmers are ideal for school bass.

CHAPTER 6

The Small Rod

At first the outfit may seem suited more for crappies than striped bass. Surely, one might say, even a 20-inch bass would double over that little fairy wand with its four-pound line. Yes, you'd be right in your appraisal, but that's the fun of it.

With striped bass fishermen being conservation minded more than ever, we thought a chapter on ultralight fishing might be needed to make those days when only the little guys are around more enjoyable.

The tackle we're writing about is a five-and-a-half-foot spin rod rated for two to six-pound line and lures up to one-quarter ounce. A tiny spinning reel like the Penn 450SS with four-pound mono completes the picture. On such a rod an eight-pound bass will fight like a 30-pounder on heavier stuff. Other species you might bump into in your travels will do likewise. A 10-pound blue will tie you up for 10 minutes - at least, while an eight-pound green bonito just won't give up.

Several lures are available, though the ones I recommend are the three-inch, plastic, minnow swimmers from Rapala, Red Fin, Rebel and Bomber. These lures float at rest but dive when cranked back with a moderate retrieve. Between the lures and line use a three-foot leader of 15- or 20-pound mono.

The small swimmers can be tossed into jetty fronts or rocky points or, in the spring of the year, into all the nooks and crannies of tidal rivers and bays. Target rockpiles, sand bars, creek entrances, small inlets, undercut sod banks or any other place spring bass stalk their prey. The first bass of the year may not be large but, on this type of tackle, they'll bring a smile some April Saturday.

As the season warms and some eight- to 15-pounders move in, the length of time needed to land a fish increases. A 15-pound bass will zip off line faster than your tax bill is going up. All you can do is hang on and hope the fish doesn't find a rock or piling to cut you off on, something that's inevitable with some fish.

We've seen folks cast the small rods from atop 25-foot boats backed into a spring beach but also seen a variety of other craft at work. Some people like tin boats and some like canoes or jon boats. A couple of enterprising souls put inflatable boats to work, the latter sometimes being towed by an early 15-pounder. A few crafty fishermen use small boats to get to shore spots inaccessible to even a four wheel drive vehicle. Remember that sand bar that's shallow enough to wade once the tide drops? You can reach it with a small boat, then fish the productive dropoff with your small rod and a pair of waders. Other boat/shore spots are islands, distant points of land or around bridges in areas that don't allow casting from atop the span. If the bridge borders a shallow bay, don't overlook bass moving up into that bay on the incoming tide. You, your boat and ultralight rod should be right behind them.

As the fishing year unfolds, don't be afraid to try the little rod if you come upon a school of bunker being harassed by blues. You can get the blues to look

Try the fast-cranking technique on some overcast day when schoolies will not respond to other methods.

Rocky points like this are ideal locations for small rod fishing for spring stripers.

at your small offering by casting the swimmer into the school, then reeling the lure back to you as fast as you can turn the handle. The small plug will zip through the bait, causing them to scramble out of the way. This scrambling creates a clear line of sight for blues, watching the bunker from below, to see your plug. It may seem crazy but those blues do, at times, grab the three-inch lure, zipping about in the midst of dozens of one-pound bunker.

With the fast-cranking technique, a speedy lure goes by so fast they don't have any time to study it. They must grab it or watch a meal get away. You can use this wrinkle to your advantage some overcast day when school bass in shoal water will not respond to more conventional methods.

As the bass population rebounds, don't be surprised to find school fish up on top under birds chasing small bait. The classic scene of bassfishing is yours to enjoy again, this time with a rod tailored to the size of the fish. However, if you happen on a school of 30-pounders, you might opt for your Danny plug rod.

The tiny hooks on the swimmers will penetrate a bass' mouth quickly - if you've kept a good point on them. To extract these hooks to assure the survival of the fish, a pair of small, needlenose pliers is right handy. Once the hooks are out, grab the fish by the lower jaw, then deposit it back in the water. The future of your fishing is in your hands. After the fish is gone, you can catch another bass on the rod the brother-in-law thought too light even for hatchery trout.

CHAPTER 7

Dropback Method

We stood on the stern of the 26-foot charter boat *Viviene*, stemming the incoming tide in one of the rips off Montauk, New York, called the Elbow. Captain John DeMaio was in the process of showing the three of us who chartered his boat how to catch bass on six-ounce jigs in 30 to 50 feet of water without resorting to wire line. Since that day I've used the dropback method, or the heave and haul as it's called in Montauk, in a variety of situations.

The procedure used is to keep a boat in gear, maintaining enough rpms to position the craft a certain distance uptide from a curling rip. Two or more anglers, depending on the beam of your boat, will lower single-hook jigs into a running tide, keeping fingers on the spool to prevent overrun. The jigs used were the A series, a style jig somewhat broader and flatter than the standard four-sided diamond jig. The flatter face of the A jig causes it to swim side to side when retrieved.

As the jig sinks, you must maintain the feel through your hand on the conventional reel (spinning is out for this type fishing) as the lure descends. As soon as it hits bottom, put the reel in gear then take five slow turns of the handle. It's important that you engage the reel the instant the lure touches down. The jig must "bounce" smartly or the effectiveness of the process is greatly reduced.

Fish generally lay just downtide of the rip, watching the current for bait being swept in the tumbled waters where they are easy prey. Your jig then is but another piece of bait. As it touches the bottom, the downward motion catches the eye of the fish holding nearby, if you've positioned the boat correctly in the tide, when you engage the reel, the lure touches down then begins to rise upward, swimming side to side as it does. A gamefish must grab the piece of bait or risk losing it in the tide.

If there are no hits on the first contact with the bottom, take the reel out of gear and drop back a second time. Keep repeating the procedure until the lure is too far away to effectively set the hook or is downtide from the fish.

The key to the operation is the feel of the lure in the tide. You must develop that feel or you will not catch well. If the tide is horsing, you may go up to eight ounces, but a heavier jig isn't the answer to maintaining proper feel; instead, try lighter line. Thirty-pound test is fine for most applications, though you'll be even more in touch with your technique with 20 or even 15-pound. The range of jigs commonly used for dropback fishing is two to eight ounces, though the four and six-ounce models are the workhorses.

Since that first exposure to the dropback 15 years ago, I've used it or a variation to catch stripers from a rock jetty bordering a deep inlet, blues from rubbly bottom in water 50 feet deep, codfish on wrecks and tarpon in the running tide in the channels of Key West Harbor. The basic idea of dropping a lure back to the bottom then reeling it slowly upwards for a short distance is one that fools gamefish more times than not.

The jigs used were the A series, a style broader and flatter than the standard four-sided diamond jig. The flatter face causes it to swim side to side when retrieved against the tide.

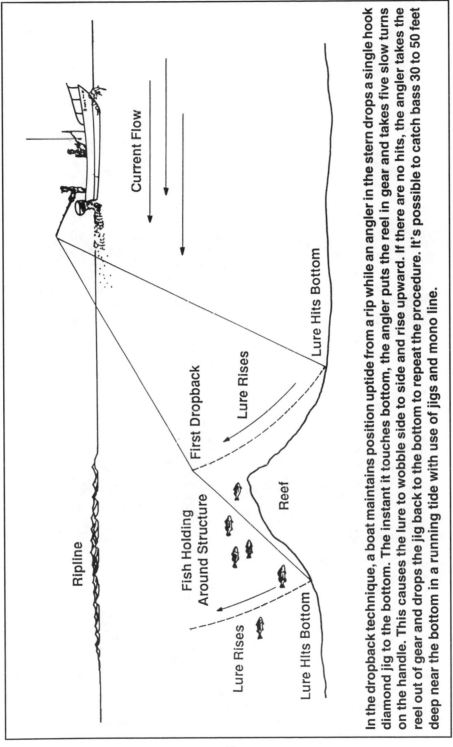

In the dropback technique, a boat maintains position uptide from a rip while an angler in the stern drops a single hook diamond jig to the bottom. The instant it touches bottom, the angler puts the reel in gear and takes five slow turns on the handle. This causes the lure to wobble side to side and rise upward. If there are no hits, the angler takes the reel out of gear and drops the jig back to the bottom to repeat the procedure. It's possible to catch bass 30 to 50 feet deep near the bottom in a running tide with use of jigs and mono line.

Current Flow

Ripline

Fish Holding Around Structure

First Dropback

Lure Rises

Lure Hits Bottom

Reef

Lure Rises

Lure Hits Bottom

Captain John DeMaio and Phil Wetmore with a bass caught in the rip off Montauk called the Elbow. That day bass were caught in 30 to 50 feet of water without the use of wire line, with A series jigs and the dropback method or the heave and haul as it's nicknamed at Montauk.

The dropback method for catching stripers in rips is best suited to the deeper areas, perhaps the edges of a rip where the water is 30- to 50 feet deep. Perhaps there are places on the Cape May Rips off New Jersey or the Nantucket Rips off Massachusetts or the North Rip off Rhode Island where the dropback method can be put to work. On our first day at Montauk, three of us boated seven bass from 20 to 34 pounds plus assorted bluefish without the wire rods.

Tackle for the dropback technique should be roughly 30-pound class blank with 3/0 or smaller reel. Conventional reels with a level wind aren't the best because the bar gets in the way of keeping your fingers on the reel, both to maintain proper feel and keep the spool from overrunning. The live bait rod we wrote about earlier could be double-dutied as a jigging stick, though somewhat longer rods have a hook-setting edge.

In between line and jig, it might be best to use a three to five-foot section of 50 pound leader. Join the main line to leader by forming a double line out of the main line with a spider hitch, then join the double line to leader with surgeon's knot. If possible, avoid bulky swivels.

There's another way to use the dropback method; this one involves bucktail jigs dressed with either pork rind or plastic worms. Let's say blues or bass are holding in a certain area, perhaps an offshore lump or just some hard bottom. You can drift over them, catching as you go, without wire line, providing conditions are right. Number one, if fish are somewhat concen-

The Montauk dropback method can be used to fool bass and other gamefish in a variety of locations.

The dropback method can also be used to catch blues and bass with bucktail jigs and pork rind.

Proper position of the hands on the reel as the lure is descending. This feel is necessary so that the angler is aware the instant the lure touches bottom.

trated, and two, there's moderate tidal flow, you can bring the dropback method to bear. Drop a bucktail of enough weight to tend bottom down to the bottom. Once it touches down, once again put the reel in gear and take five slow turns of the handle. And, once again, this means the lure descends in front of a fish then begins to swim away with the pork rind or plastic worm waving its life-like tail in the fish's face.

Blues may hit as the lure drops through them while bass usually take a bite on the upswing. Hits from even jumbo bass are sometimes nothing more than a slight tap as they inhale the lure from below. The method can also be used with heavier metal jigs to catch cod and pollock on wrecks that dot the sea floor of the northeast. It's important to vary the weight of the bucktail to the strength and ebb of the tidal flow. The lightest jig that will tend bottom is the one that will catch the best. This statement holds true for cod jigging in New England to jigging amberjacks off the southern wrecks. If you've caught well with, say, a one-ounce lure on slack water, you might have to go up to a three-ounce lure as the tide increases. This method, however, isn't suited to the boiling tide of rips; that's best left to the stemming mode of the productive dropback method.

Kerry Douton, second generation charter captain and tackle innovator, with a wire outfit made up with Penn reel, Lamiglas blank, dacron backing and 300 feet of 40-pound stainless wire.

CHAPTER 8

Basics of Wire

Somewhere in the life cycle of a bassfisher, he or she will confront the use of wire line. It's not the insurmountable devil many first timers think it is. Wire can be an effective tool in the hands of the advanced amateur, while the pros are surgically precise in their presentations.

To help one make the jump from newcomer to midranks, we asked Captain Kerry Douton of J&B Tackle in Niantic, Connecticut, for his thoughts. Kerry is a tackle innovator par excellence and a second-generation charter skipper. He cut his teeth as a mate teaching customers the use of wire line. Today, he's taken that hard-won knowledge to the floor of his tackle store and, graciously, the readers of this book.

Most striper people today use either the Penn 112H or 113H or the Diawa 300 or 400H reels. They hold a sufficient amount of backing plus the needed amount of wire. Over the years these reels have stood the test of many hours on station from Maine through Maryland.

Some anglers prefer a custom wire rod right from the start while others like the ease and cost of a factory rod. Penn Fishing Tackle Company makes two rods Kerry recommends for most northeast needs: the 2621RTC and 2701RTC. Coupled with any of the above reels, these rods become an effective starting point or will please even some 20-year charter fishermen.

If you prefer a custom stick, Kerry recommends the Lamiglas BT-85-7S blank. To build the rod you'll need six ME carbide guides plus a #16 Aftco roller tip or a #16 MD top. Completing the parts list are a #22 Fuji gimbal, seven-inch foregrip and 12-inch hypalon butt grip and a FPS 22 Fuji reel seat. Starting from the foregrip, the guide sizes are an 18, followed by a 16, two 14s, two 12s and then the tip. The guide spacing follows, starting from the tip and working back toward the reel seat. Distance between the tip and first guide is five inches; between first and second guides, five-and-one-quarter inches; second to third is six-and-one-quarter inches; third to fourth is seven-and-one-quarter inches; fourth to fifth, eight-and-one-half inches and fifth to sixth, 11 inches.

Next step in assembling your outfit is the backing. Kerry and several other charter skippers like 50-pound dacron. Fill the reel about two-thirds full, then add the wire. Different areas call for different amounts of wire. People fishing shallower areas might only need 100 to 150 feet of wire on their reels, while others prefer 300 feet or a full shot as it's nicknamed by some. Still others, namely fishermen in Massachusetts, stream 400 to 500 feet of wire to catch stripers and blues in the deeper water of Cape Cod Bay.

The average angler will use a 75-pound barrel swivel between the backing and the wire. Use a clinch knot to attach the dacron to one eye of the swivel and a haywire twist to attach the wire.

After putting on the 50-pound dacron backing, the wire is joined to the backing with a 75-pound barrel swivel. The wire is then wound on the reel evenly and under pressure so that it is packed lightly on the reel.

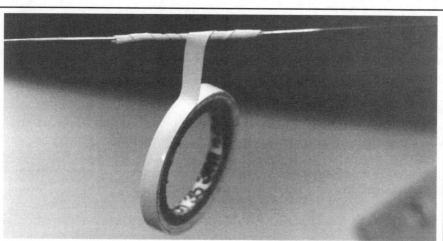

Wire line must be marked so the angler knows how much he or she has out so the lure can be riding at the proper depth. One of the best ways to mark wire is with rolls of 1/4-inch wide plastic tape. Wind the tape around the wire one way then back over itself.

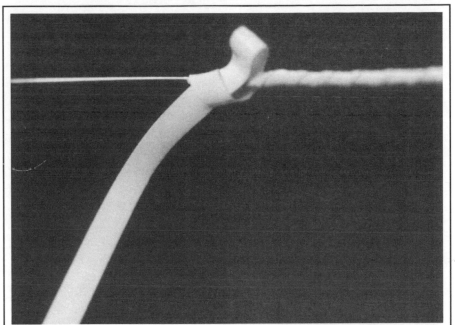

When you're done winding the tape, make a half hitch and pull tight in place then closely trim the excess.

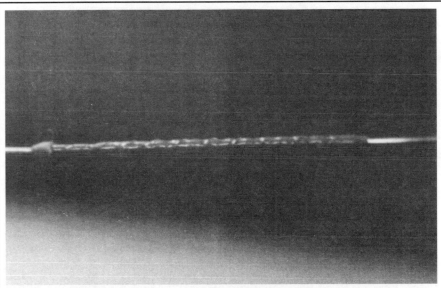

It's standard practice to use different color tape to mark the wire at intervals of 50, 100 and 200 feet. A lot of anglers favor red, white and blue for those purposes.

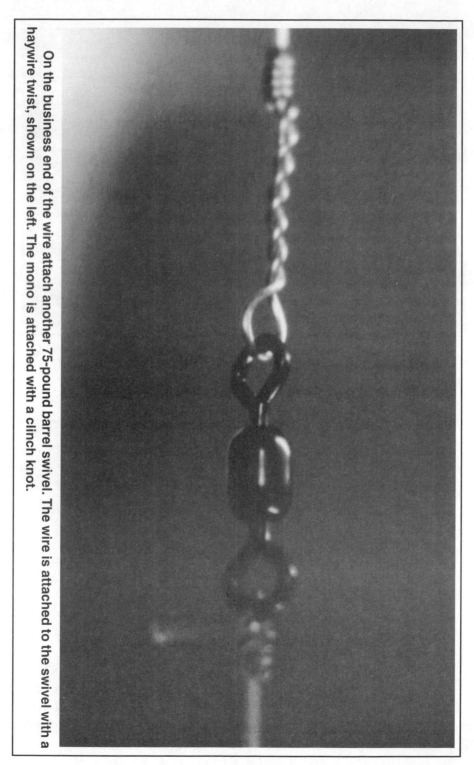

On the business end of the wire attach another 75-pound barrel swivel. The wire is attached to the swivel with a haywire twist, shown on the left. The mono is attached with a clinch knot.

It's a must to wind the wire evenly on the reel and, conversely, make sure you keep your thumb on the spool as you let the wire out. Failure to do either will result in the mother of all backlashes.

Some fishermen like monel wire because it's softer, but Kerry favors 40-pound stainless for his customers and charterboat operations. While the stainless is springier and somewhat harder to handle, it will take more abuse than the softer monel. It's recommended for beginners and used by many pros.

On the business end of the wire use the same 75-pound barrel swivel jto join it to 15 feet of leader. When you make the standard Haywire Twist, you'll always have a tag end of wire left over. If you clip this with a pair of snippers, it will leave a sharp end to cut your fingers. A safer way to remove the tag end is to hold the knot with pliers then rotate the tag end in a clockwise direction. It will break smoothly.

As to leader, most anglers favor 50, 60 or 80-pound mono for the invisible connection between lure and wire. At this point you are ready to fish.

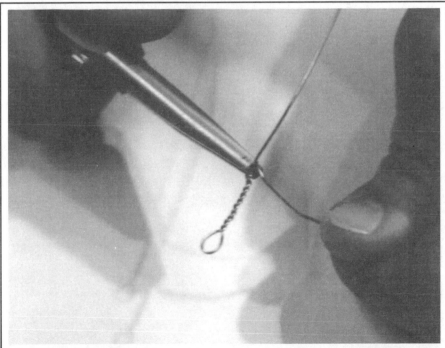

To break the tag end, hold the wire with pliers and rotate tag end in a clockwise direction until it breaks off cleanly without any rough edge.

A 14- to 16-inch red tube, spiced with a sand worm, is a daytime bass fooler worthy of every fisherman's attention.

CHAPTER 9

Tube and Worm

Here's a neat little gadget bass chasers can use whether they fish in Cape Cod Bay, the hump at Great Eastern off Montauk, or the broken bottom off Long Branch, New Jersey. Yankee fishermen call it the tube and worm. Once you get to know how to use it, I predict you'll call it effective.

What we're talking about is a 14 to 16-inch piece of red latex tubing strung with a piece of 50-pound trolling wire with barrel swivel stuck in one end and single 7/0 hook in the other. The difference between success and failure rests with hooking a juicy, whole sandworm on the stern hook, then trolling the combo down where bass hang out during the middle of the day. Obviously, the name tube and worm comes from the merging of the natural and the artificial, something regularly done in many areas to fool gamefish.

The first step to success is to secure some tubing, barrel swivels and hooks from your tackle source. Tubing with a seven-sixteenths diameter is right for most folks. Cut the tubing into the right length then put a small notch in one end. This notch will hold the hook in place. Your wire supply can come from the last trip when your brother-in-law messed up one of your wire reels after assuring you he knew just how to do it. Instead of throwing the wire away, cut out the sections not all kinked up and use the good sections to string your tubes. Cut a section of wire a bit shorter than the tube, then run it through the tubing. On the end with the notch, attach a hook with a haywire twist. On the other end of the wire, attach a barrel swivel, then pull it down into the tube so only the top eye of the swivel is exposed. Black is the best and only color to use for reasons we'll get to in a jiffy.

Because the wire is shorter than the tubing it will have a tendency to bend back on itself. The bending will form a shallow, S-shape lure when

Put the sandworm on the tube's hook like this so it streams out naturally when trolled.

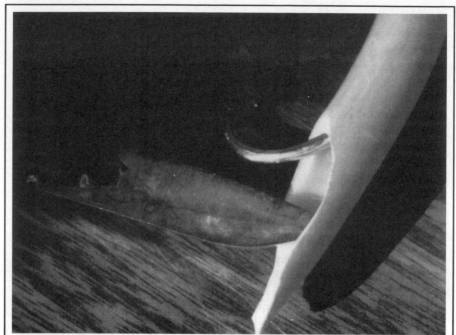

After cutting tubing to desired length, cut a notch in one end. This will hold the hook in place.

.

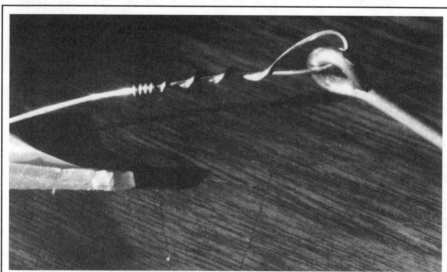

Next step is to cut some 50-pound stainless trolling wire slightly shorter than the tube. Run this through the tube and attach to a single 7/0 hook with a haywire twist.

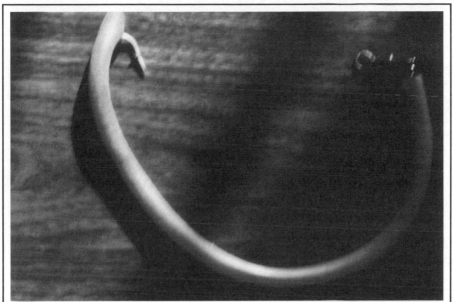

Last step in the simple procedure is to put a barrel swivel on the other end of the wire and pull it snugly down into the tube, leaving the top eye of the swivel exposed.

When not in use, tubes can be stored in a loose overhand knot. This will help them retain their fish-catching shape.

The tube and worm can fool bass lounging on offshore reefs during the summer.

trolled which, in turn, causes it to corkscrew through the water. You don't want a violent action as this entices more blues than bass. You want the lure to have a lazy motion as it's trolled SLOWLY behind your rig. To your eye and that of the fish, that corkscrew will appear as if the lure is swimming side to side, but it's only an optical illusion. If you have a boat with a big block engine, you may have to hang a five-gallon bucket over the side to slow you down. Bass are lazy creatures. The easier you make it for them to catch something their senses tell them is good, the more hits you'll receive for taking the time and trouble to read this book.

We might mention some anglers take the rigging step a bit further. Instead of one strand of wire, they braid two or three together with the aid of a variable speed drill. Once braided, they are used to string the tubes. A few anglers put a small egg sinker around the wire (to help go a bit deeper), then run the wire through the tube. If the wire will not go around the sinker, try wetting it with Lux Liquid. It will slip around the weight with ease. Note: while you have out the Lux, why not score some points with the better half? Tell her you'll do the dishes so she will not get mad when you and your partner bang around in the garage at 3 a.m. on Saturday prior to a day of striper trolling.

Once you've gotten your tubes together, find a bait source with sand-worms the size of your last tax bill. Run one of those on the hook by inserting the point into the bait about an inch or so behind the head and running the hook point forward, not to the rear. The worm will stream in a natural manner, trailing behind the end of the tube.

Next, take your wire rod and tie a tube on the end and head for the bass grounds. Before we start, we should add a couple extra items. If you have

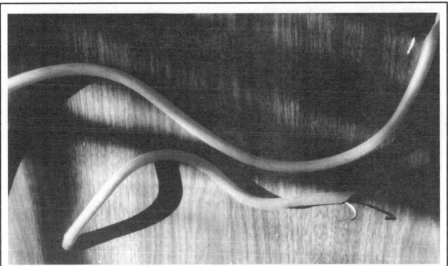

The length of the tube can be varied to suit the size of the fish. Nine to 11-inch tubes are fine for schoolies while 20- to 24-inch models are aimed at 50-pounders.

Sometimes jumbo porgies (scup) will hit a tube and worm meant for bass.

your sights set on mostly smaller fish, like in tidal rivers in the spring, the tubes can be shortened to reflect the smaller fish. If you happen to know where some 50-pounders hang out, lengthen the tubes to 24 inches. It may look like the biggest worm in creation, especially when loaded with the real thing, but that's the idea. I'll bet some bass will not know what to make of a creature about two feet long that looks alive and smells like a sandworm. I'll bet some of them will try to eat the creature.

Your bass grounds should be a place the bass will be at a given time of day. If it's early a.m., Jersey guys or gals might troll the tube and worm along the fronts of the prolific Humpback jetty or, perhaps, around Brown Avenue in Spring Lake. Rhode Island anglers might yank a 35-pounder from the reefs in front of Sakonnet Point. As the day wears on, the smart fisherman might shift his attention to the reefs offshore or some spot with deeper water where bass lounge around during the heat of the day. Because the light intensity is greatest then there's more opportunity for a bass to look over what's gyrating past its domain. You don't want anything shiny to alert the fish, hence a black swivel instead of a chrome one at the head of the lure.

Since wire line sinks about 10 feet for every 100 feet in the water, you'll gauge your wire to put the tube/worm within three to five feet of the bottom as you make a pass over the top of that offshore reef. The slowly moving combo will enter into a bass' line of sight soon after you mark fish on your fishfinder. The tube will rotate along, looking like a skinny being that's an

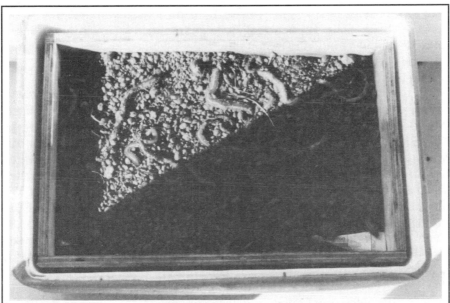

Homemade plywood worm box fits in a cooler. With the lid on, worms can be kept cool and out of the sun. The worms are stored in a mixture of Buss Bedding and saltwater spread over a couple pieces of newspaper.

easy mark. The scent of the worm usually triggers the feeding instinct. Bass do not have to expend too much energy to make a score.

Sometimes the hit will be a wallop with a solid hookup. Other times they'll bump the combo two or more times before they get hooked. I think they get a piece of the worm on such occasions, then return for more. Humans don't seem to be able to eat just one potato chip; bass do likewise with a piece of juicy sandworm.

While anglers trolling a straight up and back pattern over noon-day structures will succeed, I think the man who turns his boat, thus dropping his lure in on the fish, then turns again to pull the offering away, after they've had a look and sniff, will succeed even more. Remember, the line on the inboard side of a shallow turn toward the structure will go deeper than the rod on the other side. If you like the person on the outside rod, tell him or her to lengthen the wire somewhat as you turn. If your brother-in-law is rubbing it in about his poker winnings, say nothing. His lure will be high all day. He can clean out the blues while you mysteriously hook yet another striper.

Turning the boat, then pulling the lure back as you straighten up, takes a bit of practice. Be prepared to snag bottom as you experiment with different reefs. The loss of a few tubes and the aggravation such practice causes is worth it once you find where bass lay along that reef.

The tube/worm will also catch blues (some alligators, at times), jumbo porgies, and an occasional fluke. The motion and scent are attractants to whatever lurks around the rockpile. Once you're done for the day you can keep your tubes in their best shape by tying them in a loose overhand knot. Make sure you check each tube periodically for signs of stress. If the wire looks kinked or brittle, throw it away and restring the tube. Fifty-pound bass will hit these creations. You want your lure ready to withstand the first freight train rush should you have such a fortunate collision.

On days the fish are snappin' it's easy to run out of worms if you've boarded your rig with only one box. My friend Charley Soares of Swansea, Massachusetts, would have a flat of worms onboard most days we've tubed the New England bass. Charley, an inventive guy, built a plywood worm box that fit inside an inexpensive cooler. Charley would fill milk containers with water, freeze and then use those as coolant. He would then put his homemade insert into the cooler which would, in turn, rest atop the frozen milk containers. Into the insert Charley would lay a mat of newspaper, then a mixture of Buss Bedding and saltwater. He'd then place the seaworms in this mixture, put the lid on the cooler and store this ideal, frugal setup up inside the spray hood of his center console. When we were done fishing, he'd lift the insert out of the cooler, change the newspaper and store the rest of the bait in an old refrigerator down in his cellar. Note: It is not recommended to store worms in the upstairs refrigerator unless your brother-in-law is a good divorce attorney – assuming he's forgiven you for catching all those bass to all his blues.

CHAPTER 10

Trolling Worms

Bass anglers in the western reaches of Long Island Sound, on both the North Shore of Long Island and the Connecticut side, use a worm-fishing technique that can easily be exported to other areas. Using small boats powered by either a small outboard, electric trolling motor or an ash breeze, these fishermen troll a whole sandworm in tight to the shoreline - and catch a bunch of fish in the process.

The technique is simplicity itself. Either a conventional or spinning outfit with a 15 to 20-pound line is used to trail the worm astern. On to the working end, tie a claw style baitholder hook in sizes anywhere from #2 to 4/0. That might sound like a small hook for stripers, but the idea is to make the hook hard to see, thus increasing the worm's appeal,

After running the hook through the head of the worm, you want only the point showing out of the underside. The smaller hooks also decrease the chance of ripping the worm apart prematurely while it's being trolled. Anglers differ on length of line to be let out but 75 to 200 feet will do in most situations. Once you have the worm out behind your rig, you slowly troll along in tight to all your favorite striper haunts. Since there's no wire or drails used, you'll see right away worm trolling is a shallow water affair. One regular told me if you're in more than 15 feet, go to some other method.

The key to successful presentation is slow going. Sometimes even a small outboard on the back of a 14-foot tin boat is a little too "peppy" for worm trolling. That's where the electric trolling motor comes in. With it mounted on the stern, you can go quietly along a sod bank in a bay or along a beach that has plenty of boulders or purr along the front of a jetty. Because you just have a hook and worm behind you, you can easily stop the motor and let the worm settle into a somewhat deeper pocket. The slow sink rate of the worm makes it a tantalizing tidbit as it slowly wiggles downward.

One some nights, with the breeze canted the right way, you can work an entire shoreline courtesy of Mother Nature. The skeg of your outboard can be turned this way or that to act as a rudder when the wind cooperates nicely. If the wind is too strong, you can motor up against it, all the while maintaining the s-l-o-w speed necessary for effective worm trolling.

Worm trolling can be done in the day or with the owls. During the daylight it's in your interest to drop down a notch in your pound test. The lighter the line, the more hits. But, the lighter the line, the less chance you'll land as many fish, particularly in bony neighborhoods. That briar patch of rocks along the South Shore of Massachusetts or the front of the Humpback Jetty in New Jersey or the oceanside of Fisher's Island off the Connecticut shore or the rock-bound points between Port Jeff and Matinecock Points on Long Island hold 30-pounders from time to time that will delight in sawing 15-pound mono off on the rocks after they had your worm for breakfast.

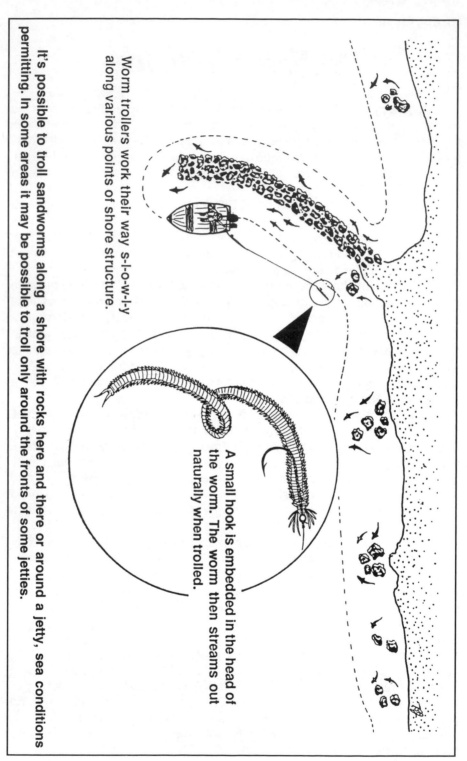

Worm trollers work their way s-l-o-w-l-y along various points of shore structure.

A small hook is embedded in the head of the worm. The worm then streams out naturally when trolled.

It's possible to troll sandworms along a shore with rocks here and there or around a jetty, sea conditions permitting. In some areas it may be possible to troll only around the fronts of some jetties.

-64-

Other critters will take a shine to your juicy sandworm. Don't be surprised if a blackfish hits the bait after you drop it down into a hole beside a rock. If you're slow trolling a worm outside the surf line along a sandy beach, a fluke, or perhaps a bluefish, will latch on. The blues can be a nuisance at times, especially the snappers. During the August full moon, Long Island Sound snappers make pests of themselves as they take worm after worm off hook after hook.

To fish the worms, it might be best to put the rod in the holder. Watch for hits but don't take it out unless the pole is down and the bass hooked. Sometimes a keeper bass will take the worm in one swipe but, other days, schoolies will bump the bait a couple of times until they eat their way to the hook. Most of the bass you'll get with worms will be smaller fish but don't complain about the 40-pounders.

In these days of catch and release, the small, single hook in the worm can be easily extracted from a fish's mouth. If the bass swallowed the hook, the line can be easily cut; the hook will rot away in time.

Most serious wormers buy worms by the flat. They store them in a variety of ways, not the least is the system described in Chapter 9. Setting out to fish either the tube and worm or to troll worms with a box of one dozen is akin to going to a double feature with four pieces of popcorn. It can be done, but it makes for a long showing. Just about the time you locate some fish, you might be out of ammo.

Long used to catch bass of northern New Jersey and western Long Island, the use of bunker spoons has spread to New England.

CHAPTER 11

Bunker Spoon Primer

From northern New Jersey and the south side of Long Island comes a platter-like lure, the bunker spoon. Long a tool of the sharpies east and south of the Verrazano Bridge, the outsize spoons are gaining attention in other areas of the striper's coast.

Measuring approximately 10 inches long by four inches across, the bunker spoon is meant to imitate a baitfish like pogies (bunkers), herring and, at times, juvenile weakfish. As you might expect with bait that size, the bass that spoons will fool will be large enough to engulf same. A couple years back, Catherine Delano landed a 68-1/2 pound bass on a Reliable bunker spoon on the oceanside of Fisher's Island. While that bass was one of the premier spoon fish, many other jumbos were fooled by these lures during the summer and fall of 1990. The area of activity stretched from Cape Cod down through the jetty row of northern "Joisey."

To get a handle on fishing spoons, we talked and fished with Mr. Russ Wilson of Neptune, New Jersey. Russ has lived and fished along the Jersey shore all his life. During his 40 years of bassfishing he's thrown or trolled everything this side of the cedar plug at stripers. In the course of that experience he's formed dos and don'ts about spoons.

To fish lures from such companies as Reliable Lure and Crippled Alewives, Russ favors nine-foot-plus rods customs built by Julian Tackle

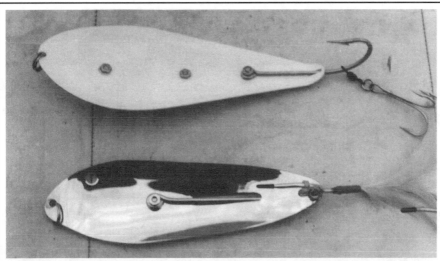

Fishing with bunker spoons is gaining popularity along the striper's coast. Show here, from the top, are: Reliable Lure Company and Crippled Alewive Lures.

Spoons have long been popular on the bass grounds on the south side of Long Island and along Jetty Row in northern New Jersey. Here master bass angler Russ Wilson is fighting a fish that grabbed a spoon off the "high rise" at Monmouth Beach. Russ and other regulars like custom built, soft action, nine-foot-plus rods for bunker spoon trolling.

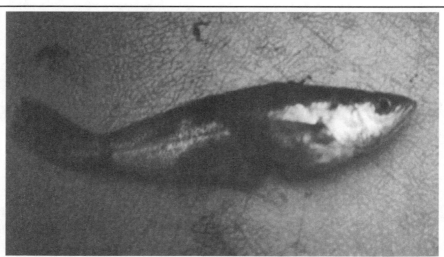

Bunker spoons are meant to imitate such baitfish as bunkers, herring and even juvenile weakfish such as this one that was spit up by a hooked bluefish.

Company in Highlands, N.J. The longer rods have a softer action that causes them to bounce and dip as the lure swings to and fro, thereby complimenting the action of the lure. Some factory rods will work okay with spoons but others with stiffer tips reduce the pronounced swing of the lure, thereby hindering its motion.

Custom built rods are available at a lot of tackle stores in northern New Jersey and Long Island. As the spoons' popularity spreads to New England, rod builders there are fashioning their own versions. For the folks who want to forego a custom built tool, Russ recommends the Diawa SL 72C or the Penn SLC 2661-RTC as two factory products for use with bunker spoons.

With his custom rods, Russ uses 150 feet of 50-pound stainless wire strung on a Diawa 400H. Between the wire and lure he uses 15 feet of 50-pound mono leader connected to the forward split ring of the spoon with a hefty ball bearing snap swivel. After putting all the wire in the water, Russ speeds up his 25-foot Hydra Sports until the spoon starts to spin rather than rock side to side. At that point, he'll ease off the throttle a shade to adjust the rpms to proper action. The dipping and darting of the tip on the long, soft rod tells the story the spoon is working. Russ has found the 150-foot section of wire works best for him. In other areas, you may easily need more or less wire.

Because of the size of the lure and its gyrating actions, some manufacturers place a treble-hook trailer on the stern hook via a small swivel. Russ, however, removes the treble and fishes the spoon with just the large, single hook, feeling that one hook gives him a better chance for a solid purchase when a large bass or blue sights in on the gyrating bunker. It should be noted, other anglers leave the treble in place and fish right as is comes from the package. By the way, spoons aren't cheap. You can expect to pay $15 to $20 for a single spoon in most stores.

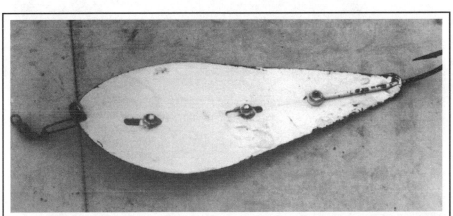

While some anglers fish with the rear treble on the spoon's main hook, Russ likes his spoons without one. He feels his chances for a solid hookup are much better with the one hook. A ball bearing snap swivel is used in the forward split ring of the spoon as a connection between leader and lure.

To get his spoon down to the right depth, Russ favors 150 feet of 50-pound stainless wire.

When conditions dictate, Russ will switch his rod from the 90 degree flush mount rod holders to this 45 degree outrigger type holder, used to keep the rod closer to the water so the spoon will run deeper.

Sometimes Russ fishes the rods in the 90 degree flush mount holders on his boat but, if conditions are such that he feels his spoons are working too high, he'll opt for a set of 45 degree outrigger type holders. The purpose of those is to keep the line close to the water, thus the spoon works deeper.

Russ trolls on land ranges much like other regulars from Maine to Maryland. He's fished the north Jersey rocks and humps so much he knows just when to turn to keep the boat over productive bottom more of the time on the water. No amount of reading can supply such local knowledge; your best bet is to observe successful anglers paying particular attention to where they're trolling their lures. If they're consistently hooking up, it's because they're putting the spoon over a reef or area of bottom that is holding the bait of the hour. Smart fishermen don't randomly troll about, hoping for a chance encounter. They're working structure of some type. And, even if that structure doesn't pay in the morning, they may return on the afternoon tide to see if bass will bite then.

Once you know the location/dimensions of a reef, you can troll over it precisely by the use of land ranges. To find out how to take a set of ranges, please turn to the next, very important chapter.

CHAPTER 12

Taking Ranges

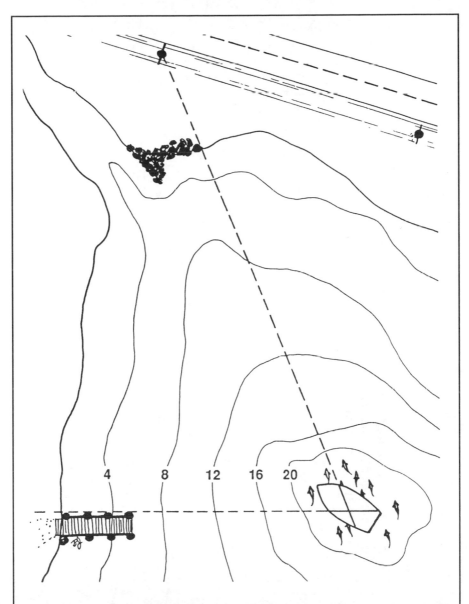

To find an inshore hot spot, you line up objects on shore. In this case, you line up the end of the rockpile with the utility pole (overhead view) and then line up the first piling on the deck with the last one.

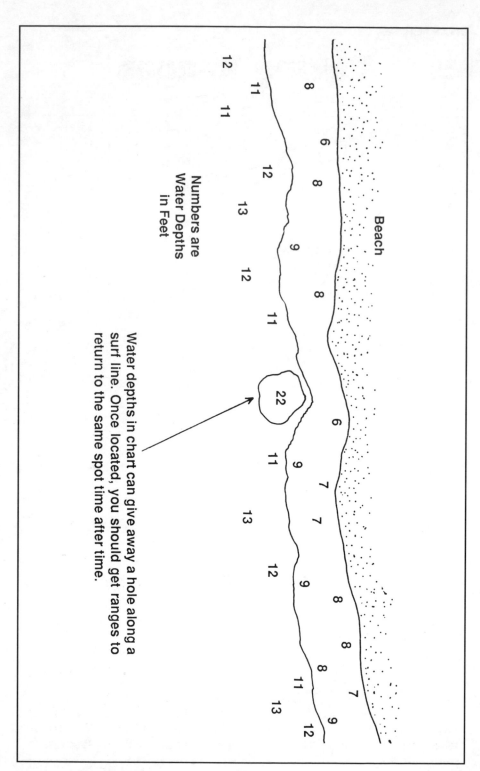

Beach

Numbers are
Water Depths
in Feet

Water depths in chart can give away a hole along a
surf line. Once located, you should get ranges to
return to the same spot time after time.

12 11 11 8 6 8 12 13 12 11 22 11 9 13 12

6 8 8 6 9 7 7 9 8 8 11 7 13 9 12

-74-

To catch bass on your new bunker spoon you must put yourself, your boat and your lures on the right lunch wagon time after time. One way is with the wonders of Loran but, lacking that, the inshore angler can do handily with shore ranges.

To revisit a bass hangout with shore ranges, an angler lines up two stationary objects on a nearby shore. The top of the funny looking building with the tip of the jetty might be one range or, in the case of our illustration, you'd line up the edge of the rockpile with the telephone pole. You could move inshore or out on that range, but the question becomes where to stop? Where along that line of sight does one find the honey hole?

Your chart recorder will give away a rise in the bottom, be it a rockpile or old dragger that now houses bass and bottom fish. As you notice the bottom coming up, look to another shore for two more objects that line up from your position on the water. In the case of our illustration, that means the tip of the outside piling with the innermost one. You now have workable ranges to return to your hole.

If, from where you are on the water, you can line up the rockpile with the pole and the first piling with the last one, you should be able to start fishing. If one or the other of those ranges is not quite aligned, move your boat until they orient themselves to your satisfaction.

Take note of which way you move your rig to get the objects on shore to change. Practice these movements until they become second nature and you'll go right to your hotspot without wasted time. If the objects on shore remain stationary, you can find the hump or wreck for the next 100 years.

Of course, you don't want to rely on objects passing by. The spiral of smoke with the girls in the lime bikini might last for the moment but not for the day. They might do as you hurriedly bring the boat about after spying something on your fishfinder en route to spot number one. It also doesn't hurt to have a marker buoy at the ready. Toss it out along with getting a temporary range, but then finalize your find with objects more reliable once it's relocated.

Most of the larger reefs are known locally and thus fished heavily. But, there are dozens and dozens of little unknown nubbins that hold a few fish. Sometimes you'll find your bass bungalow under a couple lobster pot buoys sitting off by their lonesome. Lobsters hang around structure - and so do bass so they can eat things like lobsters and all the other goodies that set up housekeeping there, too. Sometimes you'll find a spot with idle trolling if fish are spread out over a wide area. Sometimes nav markers give away a hump or, perhaps, you can seek the high spot shown on your coastal chart. If the surrounding water depths are say 25 to 27 feet and right in the middle is an 18-foot sounding, I'd take a peek at that with my tube and worm or bunker spoon. If water depths just outside Bass Beach are a uniform 10 feet, except for one spot where it drops to 22, I'd drop a live bunker in there and await results.

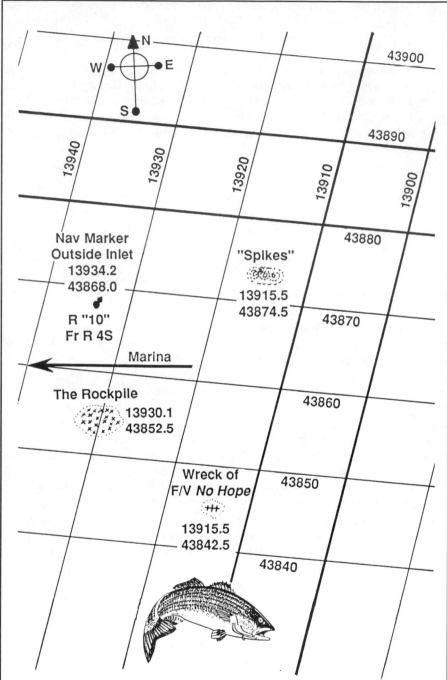

N

W ● E

S ●

43900

43890

13940 13930 13920 13910 13900

Nav Marker
Outside Inlet
13934.2
43868.0
R "10"
Fr R 4S

"Spikes"

13915.5
43874.5

43880

43870

Marina

The Rockpile
13930.1
43852.5

43860

Wreck of
F/V *No Hope*

43850

13915.5
43842.5

43840

Loran has many uses for the bass fisherman. It can aid in locating
then returning to a variety of fish-holding structures and it can help in
navigating in a fog.

CHAPTER 13

Loran Primer

We live in a world of electronic gadgets from garage door openers to our VCRs; fishing is no exception. We have increasingly compact, increasingly sophisticated fishfinders, temperature monitors, radios and, of course, Loran. In time this, too, may give way to GPS but at press time we feel the average bass hunter is more likely to have or buy a Loran than a Global Positioning System.

My first Loran was installed in a 14-foot Mirrocraft. With it I fished inshore reefs near my home without much attention. Several of the little humps and bumps I drifted eels over after dark were close to high traffic lanes. But, few gave much attention to my little rig. That suited me just fine.

I'd already had a custom wooden console built on the middle seat of the small boat for a fishfinder so it was simple work for an electronics shop to install the Loran right alongside it in the console. Folks with larger rigs will have no problem finding a convenient spot for the little box with the six-digit display. We might mention it's a good bet to have the Loran and fishfinder side by side.

Some Loran units come with a tape that will tell you how your new machine operates. All have instruction books that should be read. They will tell you how to turn the critter on and then lock in the right signal. From there it's out to the water to practice. Knowing which way to turn to get the numbers to change correspondingly takes some practice, but it can be mastered in a couple afternoons' work. If you can drive a car, you can run a Loran.

Once the unit is installed, take your boat out and notice which way the numbers rise or fall depending on how you turn the boat. A Loran is a radio

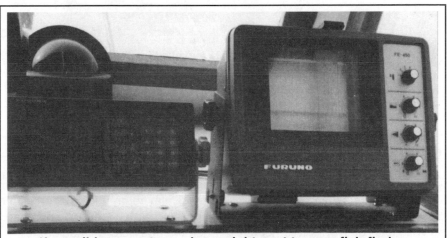

If possible, mount your loran right next to your fish finder.

Author's main use for loran was drifting on reefs at night.

receiver that takes in two intersecting signals from Loran stations at various points in the country. The receiver accepts the signals, then converts them to two, six-digit numerical displays on its face. The readout gives you your position along those intersecting lines of position as displayed on a local chart with a Loran overlay. As you change your boat's position, you change the numbers. As you motor east or north or south or west, the numbers will rise or fall.

Let's now refer to our illustration and begin work with your new toy. The chart is a fictitious example of how the Loran overlays might look on your local chart. Notice as you head to the east, the numbers on the 13-line signal decrease. As you head to the west, the opposite is true. As you run to the south, the 43-line numbers decrease; and they increase if you come about to the north.

Let's now further say you've mastered the matter of getting your boat where you want it to be. You come out the inlet and, as you head past the first nav marker, you take note its position is 13934.2 x 43868.0. Being a heads-up captain, you write that down for future reference. You then turn your attention to the "Spikes" off to the northeast. A friend gave you the numbers after seeing a couple fellows catching blackfish over what was assumed to be flat bottom. Later inspection with a fishfinder revealed some craggy stretches that might also hold striped bass.

Most Loran units will also compute distance from one point to the other. So, if you enter the numbers for the Spikes from your present position at the nav marker, it will give you a course and distance to your first stop of the day. Once arrived, you troll back and forth across the area until you get fish or strike out. Now it's time to head down to the well-known Rockpile at 13930.1 x 43852.5. This is a heavily fished area but, since it's a Tuesday, you'll chance that it might be unfished that morning. From the Spikes, you enter the number for the Rockpile and, once again, the Loran gives you course and distance.

If, in your travels, you see a hitherto unknown spike show on your fishfinder (which you alertly leave running), you can take a quick look at your numbers and spin the boat around to get more precise positioning. Tossing a

Few other anglers noticed the loran mounted next to paper machine in a 14' tin boat.

Eel fishermen can get consistent drift after drift, even on a night when it is too misty to get shore ranges, with the aid of a loran.

handy marker buoy out gives you a field of reference to backtrack systemati-
cally. A lot of bottom fish wrecks and striper haunts have been found en route
from stop one to stop two.

Our next stop is something some bass hounds may or may not know. Your
friend at the marina also parted with the numbers for the wreck of the F/V No
Hope which sank in a storm 15 years ago. Today, the remains consist of some
ribs, anchor chain and engine block, but it's structure that attracts small fish
which attract larger fish. Some of our inshore wrecks are prime grounds for
stripers just as is a reef or rip or other structure. Don't be afraid to troll your
bunker spoon or tube and worm over the ol' No Hope sitting in 28 feet of water.
Just don't get too close or you'll end up losing your tackle to the debris below.
Fish just over the wreck, not in it.

After a morning on the water, it's time to head in past the fog that rolled
in out of the southeast. Now you just put in the numbers for the nav marker and
the Loran computes the course and distance to the marker. What Loran will not
do is tell you what's headed your way.

Loran can also help you at night. My first unit had a red readout; it was
easier to see - with my eyes - than shore ranges on a misty night. It was child's
play to spend some afternoons before the bass season getting numbers on
small rips we fished before with ranges. Once you had the numbers, it meant
a short run uptide to another predetermined point ahead of the rip for the drift
back.

You can also use Loran if you troll at night. Remember the Rockpile?
There's nothing to say you can't troll a swimming plug over it once the sun goes
down just as you did a bunker spoon during the day. As you become more
proficient, you'll know at what tenth on your display a bass is likely to hit the lure.
Let's say the high spot where bass usually attack prey coming into their line of
view was our number 13930.1 x 43852.5. If you keep your boat heading north
on the 13903.1 line, that number will stay the same while the bottom will
change. Each of the tenths on your readout is equivalent to 50 to 60 feet so, if
you have 200 feet of wire astern, your lure will reach the payoff zone when
you're at 13930.1 x 43852.9. There may be other areas on the rockpile that hold
fish but the crown of the reef is usually a place to start looking.

Notice our Loran lines on our illustration conveniently cross at right
angles. The lines on your home grounds might not do the same, so you'll have
to adjust the boat movement accordingly to reach a certain area. For instance,
you may have to head slightly east-northeast to get the one line to move or,
perhaps, slightly south-southwest to get the other station to change. A buddy
versed in Loran and bribed with his choice might be a good investment on a
Saturday afternoon before the first good charge of fish show on the appropriate
spring tide. He or she can coach you on what you're doing right or wrong.

Master bass angler Sherwood Lincoln has caught over 50 bass weighing more than 50 pounds on a three-way rig.

CHAPTER 14

Three-Waying Eels

Most fishermen would part with substantial assets if they could catch a 50-pound striper. Some anglers fish all their lives without ever catching one that size. However, would you believe there are fishermen in the northeast who've caught half-a-hundred bass that size? Yes, there are. Folks like Sherwood Lincoln of Old Saybrook, Connecticut, have landed at least 50 fish over the magic 50-pound mark.

What's the secret? The answer lies in a method called three-waying. It's a glorified fluke rig that presents a large bait right down on the dinner table, right down where jumbo bass spend a good part of their lives; on the bottom. For every time a 54-inch bass crashed through a foaming breaker to grab a one-ounce popper, there are dozens more times when they grabbed an 18-inch eel drifted over a reef in 30 to 50 feet of water some night under a bright or dark moon.

Starting with this chapter and going into the next two, we'll give you the basics of three-waying. It can be used with live eels, live bunker or herring or with bucktails. First, let's address the use of eels.

Three-waying gets its name from the use of a three-way swivel which is the centerpiece of the rig. You start with a spool of 50, 60 or 80-pound mono. The size of the mono used to string the rig differs slightly with different anglers. The 50 may work if you fish in rips with smooth bottom during the light of day. If you're fishing hard, broken country, go with the 60 or 80.

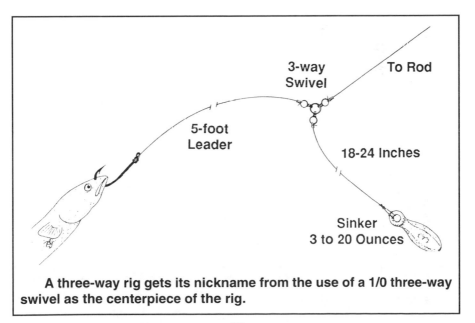

A three-way rig gets its nickname from the use of a 1/0 three-way swivel as the centerpiece of the rig.

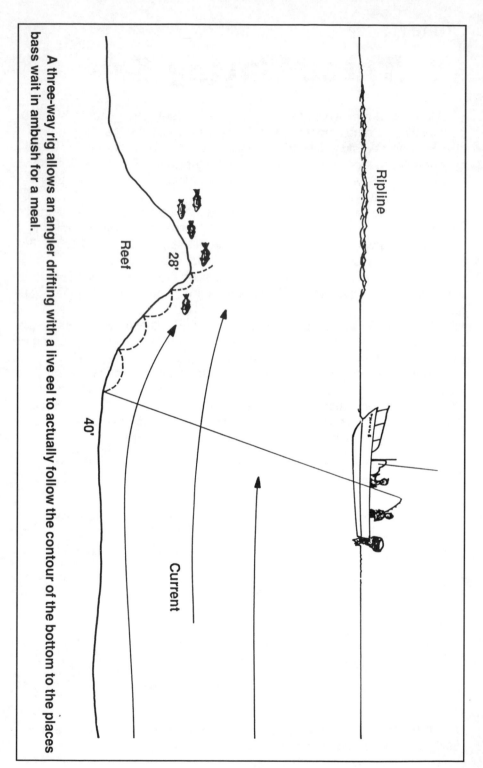

A three-way rig allows an angler drifting with a live eel to actually follow the contour of the bottom to the places bass wait in ambush for a meal.

Ripline

Reef

28'

40'

Current

To tie up the rig, get a good quality 1/0 three-way swivel, not one pulled apart by the bass of your dreams. If you set your sights on big fish, you'll have to get in the habit of appraising your tackle and rig. Ask yourself, if the next fish to eat this weighs 70 pounds, will I be ready for her? On to one eye of the swivel tie about 18 to 24 inches of mono, then put a loop on the other end. Put a sinker anywhere from three to 20 ounces in that loop. The idea of the rig is to tick the bottom in a running tide. In some places, like the Race off New London, Connecticut, this means a pound or more of lead. In other areas you can get by with the three-ouncer. The lightest sinker that will tend bottom is the rig that will catch the best. Of course, you'll have to go to more lead as the tide picks up somewhere after the first hour of flow. Conversely, you'll need to reduce the lead when it eases off – in stages – sometime after the third hour of the tide. Changing sinkers enables the rig to just tick the bottom, but not get hung up into all the time. To further prevent that from happening, it's best to take a turn of the reel handle each time your sinker touches bottom in a rocky area. On soft bottom, such precautions aren't as necessary.

Onto the second eye of the swivel, tie a five-foot section of the mono to a stout, claw-style hook. Sizes 6/0 through 8/0 should fill most needs. Tie your main line to the third eye of the swivel and you're ready to roll.

Tackle for three-waying should be all conventional; spinning doesn't have

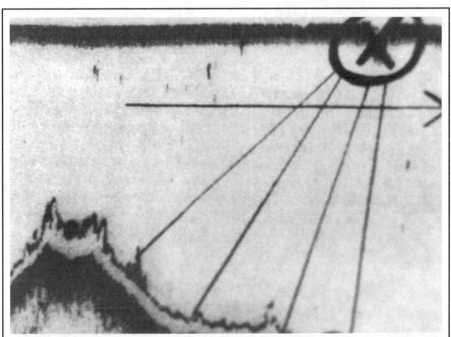

Once the crest of a reef has been cleared, the angler, here represented with an X in a circle, can follow the bottom contour by continually dropping the rig back to the bottom to a bass that may be holding on the downside of the high spot.

One of the heaviest bass ever landed was this 76-pounder caught by Captain Bob Rochetta off Montauk Point. Shown here are Bob, his daughter and Dave Motherway, Jr.

the muscle. If you're fishing areas where three to six ounces of lead will stay down most tides, then I'd go with a 20 or 30-pound class blank with a 3/0 size reel with 20 or 30 pound mono. Note: in some locations you may be able to effectively fish with a lot lighter tackle. But, if you're intent on catching jumbos from the rocky bottom around Montauk and Plum Gut, Long Island, then I follow the pros. They mostly use 40 or 50-pound mono (some prefer Dacron) on a 30 or 50-pound class blank. Reels for that type fishing are normally of 4/0 size. It takes a sturdy stick to move a rig with a 16-ounce sinker to set the hook in the tough jaw of a big bass.

Now that we're rigged up, let's go looking for some fish to put on your wall. You'll be fishing at night with eels trapped in wire mesh pots in local ponds or rivers or bought from a local bait shop. Chain stores don't carry eels. With a supply of 12 to 36 eels in a bucket, look at places like the rips to the east of Nantucket or east of Cape May. The mouth of a tidal inlet might be another spot. Sharpies regularly catch jumbo bass at the exit of the Galilee Breachway in Point Judith, Rhode Island. Breachway is a New England term for inlet and the conditions at Galilee are very similar to those found in inlets below Asbury Park on the Jersey shore. We also think three-waying might work off Sandy Hook or, perhaps, at the mouth of the Merrimack River in Newburyport, Massachusetts, or, maybe, further up in the Saco River in Maine. We saw some deep holes in the latter spot with some telltale marks on a color sounder that looked like the right stuff.

Three-waying will work any place large bass are holding in deeper water in a running tide. I'd look for depths of 30 to 60 feet on the deeper edges of some rips or, in the case of an inlet, that section of water near the mouth where bass can lie at the edge of the current watching what's coming downtide without expending a monumental amount of energy to maintain their hunting position.

Eels of 16 to 20 inches are used by most bass fishermen. Hook them under the mouth and bring the hook point out the top of the head. A piece of rag will give you a purchase on the eel's slimy hide long enough to get a hook into it.

If you're fishing a rip, run uptide from the first curl, drop your rig in, then let it bounce along as you drift back with the tide. If your sinker isn't near the bottom, change to a heavier one. The exception to that might be places where bass hold at mid-depths. One such area is the North Rip off Block Island, Rhode Island. There we'd had occasion to drop in the rig, put the reel in gear and catch fish holding 20 feet off bottom. We've also had nights when it's best to have the rig down deep.

Bass are drawn to rips because it's there the killing is easiest. A rip is formed when the tide flows up and over a hill. If the tide is moving along in 40 feet and all of a sudden runs into a rock ledge that rises to 28 feet, the water will be forced uphill. A rip will form on the surface slightly downtide of the hill. Underneath that rip, at the underwater apex of the hill, the tide will pick up steam as it's forced into a more constricted space. The sweep and speed of the tide up the hill causes a jumbled mass of swirling water and disoriented baitfish near the peak. There large bass can wait as the bait is tumbled about. With their broad tails and heavy bodies, the bass are ideally suited to maneuver into that melee to grab a meal. As you see, that 50-pounder got used to the easy living and easy pickings on that rip. The tide brings her food and the water depth gives her safety. The next thing she might grab at her 1 a.m. feeding station is your eel.

Another aspect of the three-way rig is its ability to follow the contour of the bottom. Some bass will hold down in the valley behind the small hill we've just described. As you watch your fishfinder, you'll see the bottom drop back down as you drift through the turbulent rip. Note: in some areas this may be too dangerous at the strength of the tide. As you clear the peak, you can take your

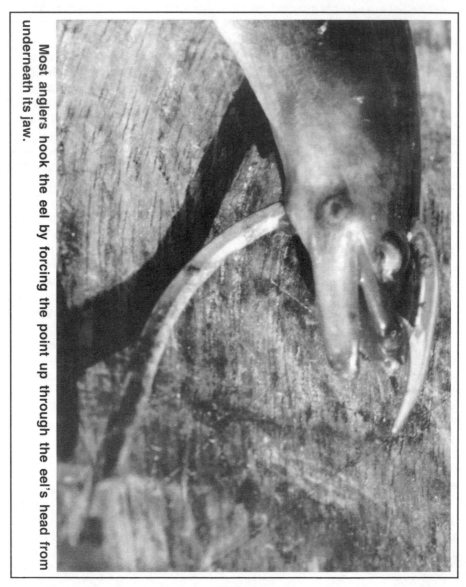

Most anglers hook the eel by forcing the point up through the eel's head from underneath its jaw.

reel out of gear and drop the rig again and again. What you're doing is walking the eel back down the hill, hopefully in front of a monster sitting there awaiting what we don't know. But, she may not refuse the tasty eel that good fortune brought within her line of awareness.

If it's too dangerous to fish a certain spot on the strength of the flow, don't overlook the slower sections of the tide. We've had stellar moments during the last hour of the ebb when current flow was a bare minimum. During such times the wise angler shortens his drift to include only the fish-holding territory. If the wind become stronger than the tide at those times, the wise fisherman also takes such into account when positioning his rig for the next drift. The angler who does the best at three-waying is the one able to put his boat over the fish time and time again. That maneuver, as the tide or wind weakens or increases, is the one that separates the highliners from the spectators.

Generally, the better fishing is during periods of stronger tides. From four days before to four days after the new and full moons are prime times. Sometimes, though, the unpredictable bass bite until the current peaks, then ease off until the current does likewise. During periods of the month with below average tidal flow, the best action may not come until the peak of the tide. Along with that, you can understand why bass drive some souls to the rubber-rod farm. Times of peak tidal flow are available in the Eldridge Tide and Pilot Book, sold in some of the larger, better marine supply houses. We should also mention high tide and the start of the current are not one and the same. It's very possible to have an ebb current start two hours after predicted high water. Those figures, too, are available in the Eldridge book, something no successful fishermen should be without.

When a jumbo bass grabs an eel in a running tide, she has to eat it quickly or it will get away. Most hits will be a sharp tap followed quickly by another. The second tap is your signal to set the hook. The first bounce told you a bass rushed over to grab its prey; the second tap was the bass hurriedly opening its cavernous mouth to inhale the creature wriggling in her grasp. After you've set the hook, the fish will thrash this way and that, trying to rid itself of the hook. When this fails, it will take off in a rush. Once she stops, slowly pump and reel as you bring line back on the reel. If the fish turns and goes a second time, you've likely got a prize beyond a 45-pounder. If you don't want the bass for eating or mounting, unhook it and let it swim away after you held it upright over the side and let water flow through its gills. You can catch it again next season, a few pounds heavier.

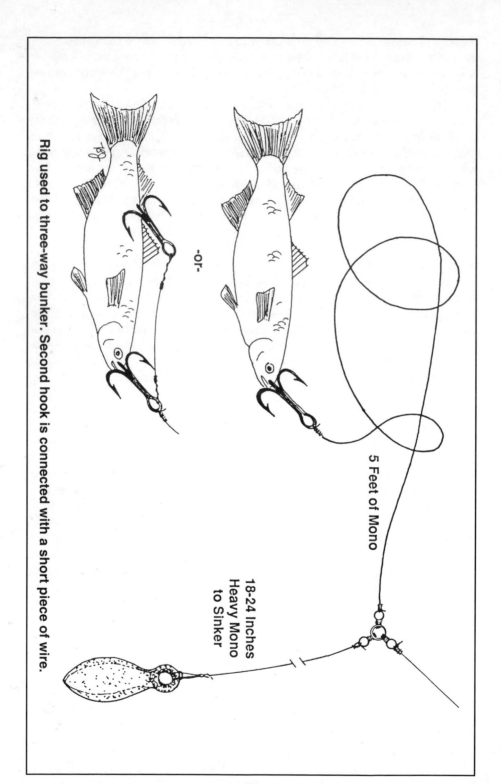

Rig used to three-way bunker. Second hook is connected with a short piece of wire.

-or-

5 Feet of Mono

18-24 Inches
Heavy Mono
to Sinker

CHAPTER 15

Three-Waying Bunker

Once you have the basic three-way rig constructed, you can do other things with it in addition to or in place of fishing at night with eels. If you like bass chasing under the light of day, there's a method of three-waying for you.

In the early parts of this book, there was a chapter on how to get a tank of live bunker (pogies in New England). Well, let's say you now have 15 or 20 frisky baits in your tank. Now what? Take your three-way rig and tie it to a single 1/0 or 2/0 treble that has been inserted through the nostrils of a bait. The nostril openings are the two small holes on the port and starboard sides of the bait's head between its eyes. Run the point through one side and out the other. Don't go too deep or you'll injure your ticket to a big bass.

Next step is to put a sinker of sufficient weight to take the bait down - and keep it down - as you drift along in a running tide. Just like with eels, you do the same thing during the day with live bait. The sinker keeps the bait down in front of the bass and the wiggly, lively bait will tempt her if she's at all inclined.

Places to look for action are offshore reefs and rockpiles, deeper edges of rips or, perhaps, the mouth of an inlet. Don't overlook the mouth of an inlet some summer day once all the morning traffic has gone to sea. If an ebb current starts around 9 a.m., it might be in your interest to drift a bunker through there. Remember to seek out that part of the current's edge where bass can watch what comes downtide without expending a lot of energy.

Fairly stout tackle is needed to handle a live bunker and weight heavy enough to get it near the bottom in a running tide.

Three-waying with a live bunker is an ideal way to fool jumbo bass right in broad daylight.

Three-waying a live bunker has produced many large stripers at locations like Race Rock Light off Connecticut and it will work in many other areas of the stripers' domain.

A common sight if blues are around when using just one treble hook in a three-wayed bunker.

Another possible productive drift pattern would be to drift the bait alongside the ice breakers of bridges or, perhaps, parallel with the rock rip-rap usually bordering inlets.

I wonder how many anglers try a three-way rig in Shark River inlet in New Jersey or, perhaps, further south in the Cape May rips. We know three-waying live bunker has accounted for hundreds of jumbo bass around Race Rock Light off Connecticut, but is it used off Race Point on the tide of Cape Cod? The deep water and strong tides there make three-waying seem a natural. How about some of the famed Nantucket Rips? Some of the inlets on the South Shore of Long Island will undoubtedly produce for the three-wayers. How about around treacherous Barnegat Inlet? There are deep holes near the North Jetty or, perhaps, around the remains of the jetty on the south side. The latter spot was always productive for jetty jockeys who waded the mussel-encrusted rocks to have bass grab lures right at their feet. Would a bunker three-wayed along those rocks produce fish? If I had ten dollars for every bass over 30 pounds that has been caught in New England over the last 25 years on a live bait on a three-way rig, I'd be sending greetings from my condo on the out islands.

It will take stout tackle to fish a one-pound bait along with a sinker heavy enough to keep it down in the tide. Aim for at least a 30-pound blank with a 3/0 or 4/0 reel. If you're fishing on soft bottom, 30-pound mono with 50-pound on the three-way might be fine. If your bass hang out in bony neighborhoods, use 40 or 50 on the reel and 60 or 80 to string your rigs.

Bluefish, bless their toothy little hearts, are a problem for the three-wayer. They love the same spots the bass hang around during the day. If, however, they grab your large bait with only the one treble in the bow, they'll likely get to have your bait without getting your point. This situation is remedied by using a second treble connected to the head one with a short piece of wire. The second treble is hooked just under the flesh shortly behind the dorsal fin. The next time Mr. or Ms. Bluefish bites, he or she gets the hook.

With the second, or stinger hook as it's sometimes called, you can set up on a bass much quicker than with a freelined bait. The hit will usually be a thump signaling a fish has rushed up and grabbed hold. The second wiggle is the fish opening her mouth to swallow her prize before it gets away. That's the time to set the hook. A 30-pounder has mouth enough to get a one-pound bunker down without a hiccup. With the quicker set, the chances are greater the fish will be hooked in the mouth, not down in the gut. That makes unhooking and releasing so much easier.

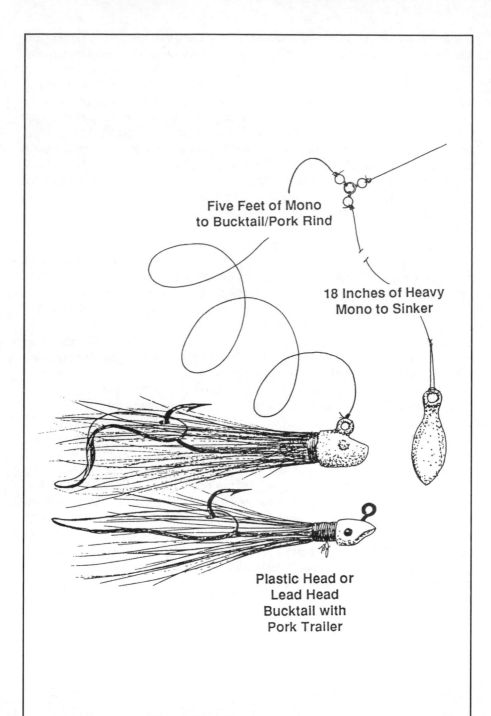

Five Feet of Mono
to Bucktail/Pork Rind

18 Inches of Heavy
Mono to Sinker

Plastic Head or
Lead Head
Bucktail with
Pork Trailer

Rig for three-waying bucktails. On top is a bucktail with plastic head and underneath it is a leadhead. Both of these are used for drifting.

CHAPTER 16

Three-Waying Bucktails

We can take the same three-way rig and add yet a third dimension to its fish-catching abilities. Instead of a single hook and eel or live bait we can add a bucktail and pork rind, yes, that's right, a bucktail/rind combo just like most bass fishermen associate with jig trolling. We will, however, drift this lure in the currents coming out of inlets or heading into a bass-holding rip.

Our rig is the same dimensions as Chapters 14 and 15; a 1/0 three-way swivel with 18 to 24 inches of 50, 60 or 80-pound mono from one eye of the swivel to a sinker heavy enough to tick the bottom in a running tide. Onto the second eye of the swivel, tie five feet of the same heavy mono and attach it to a bucktail designed for driftfishing.

Driftfishing with bucktails originated in the fast waters of the Race off New London, Connecticut. Some enterprising soul started drifting with a lure normally used for trolling - and started catching jumbo bass, both day and night. As news of the success of this method leaked out, fishermen started making improvements on the technique. The two lures that survived the process of hard knocks were either a small lead bucktail somewhere between 1/2 and 3/4 ounces that had its mold machined out to take an 8/0 hook, or bucktail made up with plastic heads, yes, that's right, plastic instead of lead.

Some expert drift fishermen like to use the small lead bucktail all the time while others favor the more buoyant plastic. Still others have time and tides they use both. It might be best to buy a couple of each, then experiment to see what works best for you.

The idea is to use a sinker heavy enough to continually graze the bottom as you drift along. The lighter weight of the smaller, lead bucktail or the

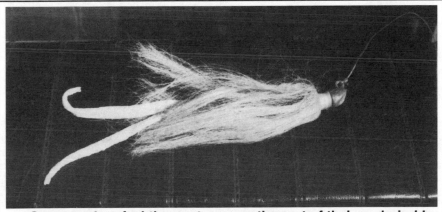

Some anglers feel they get more action out of their pork rind by splitting the tail with a pair of sharp scissors.

Bucktail with a plastic instead of lead head. These are used effectively for three-waying bucktails/pork rind. One of the beauties of using bucktails is it lets an angler fish his way through the blues.

buoyancy of the plastic head keeps the lure slightly up away from the bottom. When you add a strip of #70 Uncle Josh pork rind, you now have a lure that will dip and weave each time the sinker touches down, thus creating an undulating motion that makes the drifted bucktail look like a juicy sea creature to bass and blues. Some anglers feel they get added benefit from their pork rind by splitting it down the middle. This system is great when bass are feeding on squid or other smaller bait.

Your local tackle dealer may not have heard of this method, so you can secure literature and prices on drifted bucktails by writing to Mr. Marshal Green, Sea Link Ltd., Box 548, South Lyme, CT 06376. Fishermen in eastern Connecticut can readily locate drift bucktails in stores catering to bass fishermen. If there are do-it-yourselfers out there, most any Smilin' Bill type mold in the 1/2 to 3/4 ounce range will work provided it's machined out to accept a smaller hook. Bass to 60 pounds have been caught on this method, so don't waste time with a small hook.

As to colors, the standard drift colors in the deep water of the Race are green Fish Hair with a strip of yellow/white pork rind, with the white side down. If that combination doesn't bring any hits, or fish whacking it after a couple successive drifts, successful bassmen change over to other color combos like an all-white bucktail with white pork rind. Changing colors, especially during the light of day, can make a difference, though there's no need to have every hue of the rainbow. Green/yellow, white/white and white with red pork rind will do the trick most days. Of course, we must always be on the lookout for that color

Bass of this size are very common when three-waying bucktails during the day.

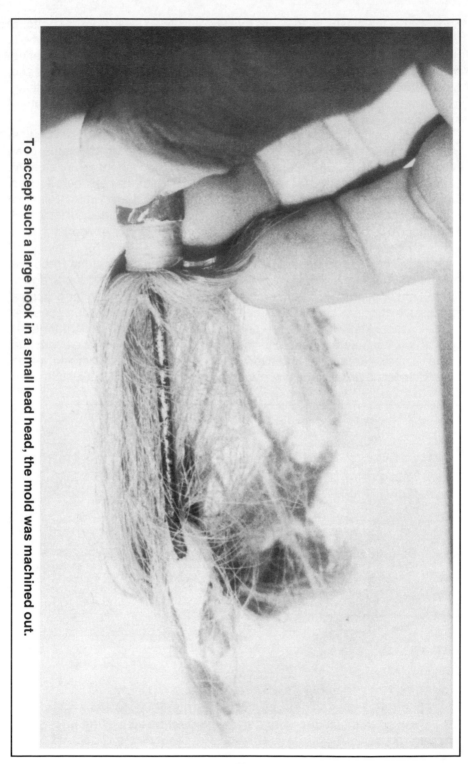

To accept such a large hook in a small lead head, the mold was machined out.

that's hot in one area but doesn't do much any place else. Above all else in fishing, never argue with success. If something's working, stick with it.

Three-wayed bucktails can be drifted in places like Great Eastern at Montauk Point or any other confluence of water where bass and blues gather. If there are any bay fishermen in the audience, you could drift a three-way rig where a feeder creek or river empties into a bay or, perhaps, an inlet or breachway or, in deeper, faster sections of rivers where depth and tricky terrain prevent the use of downriggers. As with eels and live bait, the three-way rig permits an angler to follow the contour of the bottom like a shadow.

I've often thought three-wayed bucktails would be devastating in the rips east of Nantucket and south of Monomoy Island off the tip of Cape Cod. Any place there's a collision of swift tides or water flowing up a hill over a reef has the potential to be used as a spot for three-waying.

Three-waying bucktails has the extra benefit of letting you fish through a school of blues, awaiting a bass. This saves wear and tear on your live bait supply.

Bucktails rigged in this fashion can be used both day and night though the larger bass will generally be taken after dark. Your catch during the day will usually be fish under 30 pounds and blues. When a bass grabs the bucktail drifted instead of jigged with wire line, the hit will be a sharp rap or slight tap. In any event, with some practice you'll distinguish bottom bouncing from the real thing. As with other methods of three-waying, if you're drifting on a rising, rocky bottom, take a turn on the reel each time you tap a rock, and increase or decrease the weight of the sinker as the tide flow does likewise. While the drifters in the Race might need 20 ounces of lead on the strength of some tides, there's nothing to say another angler in a New Jersey tidal estuary might not do very well with a 3 ounce sinker and plastic bucktail. From the southernmost reaches of a striper's travels to the Saco River and beyond in Maine, the three-way rig has plenty of undiscovered potential.

Some anglers might want to fish from an anchored boat rather than drift into a rip.

CHAPTER 17
Dunk a Chunk

Drifting into a churning rip isn't everyone's idea of a good time, even if it does mean catching stripers. There are plenty of fishermen out there who'd like to have a chance at catching a big bass but would like to do so from their boat anchored securely over some thoroughfare fish traverse in their daily search for food. If this type angler is you, then chunk fishing might be your game.

For every 50 pounder caught chasing a small popping plug in the surf, there's a dozen caught on a juicy chunk cut from a herring, bunker or mackerel. That chunk laying on the bottom is akin to a drifter finding a $100 bill. Hungry bass have found a piece of medium rare and usually scarf up your offering with little trouble.

Getting bait to fish with requires a little time beforehand. River herring can be netted in the spring then fished that day or frozen to use later. Frozen bait has caught lots of fish but fresh dead is of prime concern. Mackerel can be caught in quantity during their invasions, then stored away in a freezer until needed. Bunker, the most common, can be caught in numbers then frozen. All or some of the above are also sold in local stores.

The secret to catching better than the other 99 guys out chunking is chumming. If tuna anglers can toss pieces of cut fish over the side to draw the giants to their slicks, bass fishermen can do likewise. To start chumming you need a quantity of fish to cut up and toss over the side at slow but steady intervals. A cutting board and knife are also needed. The idea is to lure fish to your baited hooks, not feed them to the point they're discouraged from eating any more.

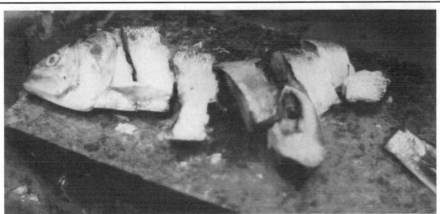

The key to fishing with chunks is chumming. Bass anglers, like tuna fishermen, can toss pieces over the side to draw fish to their hooks.

Once your boat is anchored at a highway where you think bass will cruise in their travels, cut up a couple of baitfish into five or six pieces, depending on their size. Start by tossing a handful of chunks into the running tide, then wait a bit, then toss a couple more over every so often. The trick to chumming is to toss just enough to draw the fish, not to feed them. However, once you hook up, don't forget the chum. You may hold the school with the pieces already on the bottom but, then again, the school may simply continue on with their meanderings looking for a further source of food.

The baitfish used for chum don't have to be as fresh as today's sunrise, but the fresher your hook baits, the better you'll do. That nice, juicy, dripping hunk cut out of the midsection of a fresh, dead bunker (pogy in New England) will seem a deluxe prize when found by a blue or bass drawn upcurrent to the source of the chum. If you've chummed the right way, the school of fish will linger in your area looking around for their day or night's chow.

Chumming can be done both day and night. In the daytime, it's sometimes best to move out into the deeper water where bass mill around during the heat of the day. We had stellar catches of jumbo bass in August in the 1970s fishing chunks on the bottom in 50 feet of water off Scarborough, R.I. We think Jersey anglers could put chunks to use outside jetty row in places like Monmouth Beach down to Spring Lake. Long Island anglers who frequent the south side could put anchoring and chumming to superb use. It's already practiced by Connecticut anglers in Long Island Sound and further up in Rhode Island. Folks who live and fish around Boston Harbor up through rock-bound Manchester can anchor and fish a juice chunk on the bottom. Off some towns, daytime chunkers might get more blues than bass and, off some areas at night, dogfish present a challenge.

Rigging for chunk fishing can be simplicity itself or, perhaps, a few add-ons will be needed. One trip with Mr. Fred Bova off Stamford, Connecticut,

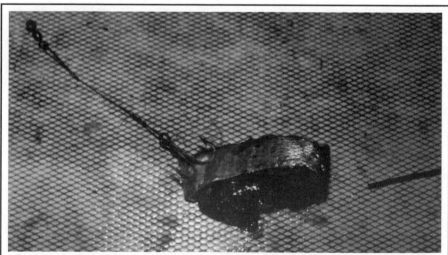

Some anglers use a small trace of wire to prevent bluefish cutoffs.

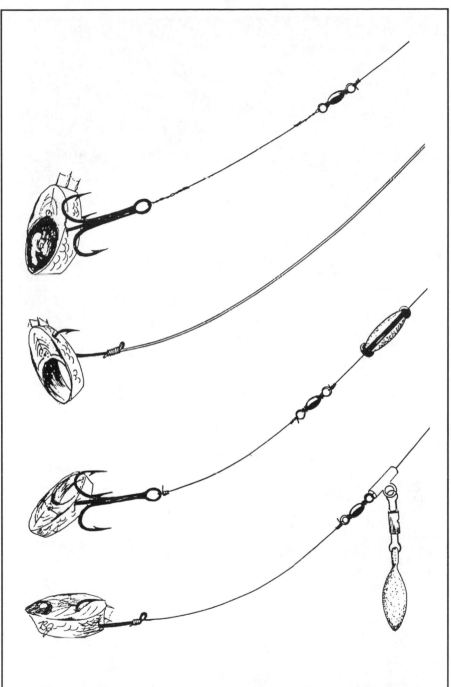

Four ways to rig a chunk bait. Top to bottom are treble hook with small trace of wire, chunk on heavier mono, small rubber core sinker up leader to get bait down in a moderate tide, and a fishfinder rig.

The bane of night chunkers in some areas is the dogfish.

showed all that was needed was a boat rod, conventional reel with 30 to 40-pound mono and a single 7/0 or 8/0 hook. Freddy hooked a fresh chunk in one end, then tossed it over the side. He took a live bunker and tossed it out on a second rod. In time a 30-pound bass came up and chased the live bait but ended up taking the easy way out; it found the fresh, juicy chunk on the bottom and had its breakfast. In other areas, people use 1/0 to 2/0 treble hooks in their chunks. Between the treble and the line, they put a small trace of wire connected to the running line with a two-way swivel. You don't need much wire, a couple inches is enough to keep a bluefish from snapping you off. If there are blues in the area you choose, don't be surprised if they rise from the bottom to hit a chunk as it barely clears your line of sight down into the water.

If the current is a factor, some folks place a small, rubber core sinker up the line from the bait. Still others use a fishfinder rig, attach a sinker heavy enough to keep the chunk on the bottom, then place either a mono or wire leader between fishfinder and chunk, then start fishing.

There's also another, specialized method of chunk fishing practiced on the reefs off Watch Hill, Rhode Island. There anglers use lead core line to fish chunks down near the rocky bottom in the running tides.

If you've chosen a rocky area to fish, I'd say stick with a single hook as it will be less prone to snag. If you're fishing softer bottom, then you can use a treble if that's your favorite hook.

After the baits are on the bottom and the chumming ongoing, put the reels in free spool with the ratchet on. When a fish grabs the bait, the noise will alert you or your fishing partners. You don't have to give much line like live bait fishing. Even a 10-pound bass will have a chunk down in no time. Set the hook, enjoy the fight, then let most of your catch swim away.

There's yet another facet of chunk fishing that deserves mention. Some anglers actually take a casting rod and flip the pieces of fish into boulders awash along a shore, just like you would a plug or other artificial lure. If bass are around that rockpile that day, they'll bite on that nice chunk dropping into their line of sight as they scan the white water. We've seen this technique practiced effectively in several places, not the least of them being the south side of famed Cuttyhunk Island.

Chunking and chumming can be deadly effective but, in this day of conservation, it should be used sparingly with regard to numbers of fish killed. If you enjoy catching those big, bright, beautiful creatures whatever God you believe in has entrusted to our care, then don't spoil your chances for good fishing the same time next year.

Your wire line outfit can be used to troll live bait as well as lures.

CHAPTER 18

Wire Line and Live Bait

Now that we've covered some of the basics of bassfishing, we can take live baitfishing a step further. Instead of drifting or trolling a bait with mono, we can now pull out the wire line rod to get our baits down deeper.

The same wire rod of Chapter 8 will do the job nicely. Onto the end of the wire put about 15 feet of 50-pound leader. Onto the end of the leader tie the same 1/0 treble we wrote about earlier. Connect the treble to a bunker through its nose, toss the bait over the side, let out enough wire to get down near the bottom, then start trolling. The wire will take your bait down closer to the bottom, closer to the zone where creaker bass spend the better part of their lives.

Trolling a bait with wire line can be effectively done off Jersey's jetty row, both sides of Long Island and all the way up into New England. As you move along slowly (the only speed for live bait trolling), you'll need to keep the reel in free spool with your hand on the spool to prevent overrun. When a bass grabs hold, let him run for a count of three or four, then set the hook.

If bluefish are a problem, with baits coming in minus their stern sections, borrow a page from the three-waying chapter and use a stinger hook. Attach another 1/0 treble with a short piece of wire to the hook in the bunker's nose, after you insert the back treble just behind the bait's dorsal fin. Next time Mr.

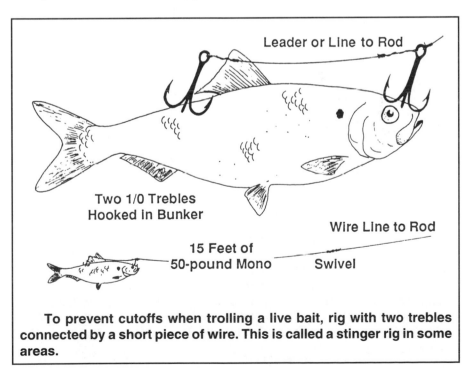

Leader or Line to Rod

Two 1/0 Trebles Hooked in Bunker

Wire Line to Rod

15 Feet of 50-pound Mono

Swivel

To prevent cutoffs when trolling a live bait, rig with two trebles connected by a short piece of wire. This is called a stinger rig in some areas.

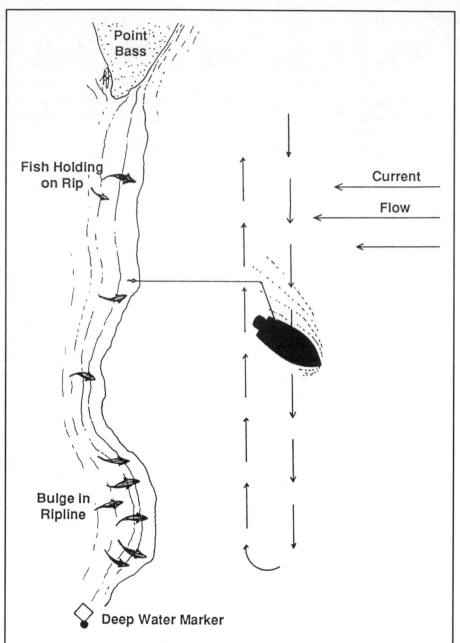

Point Bass

Fish Holding on Rip

Current

Flow

Bulge in Ripline

Deep Water Marker

When fishing a rip with wire line, you can cover maximum ground by positioning the bait just behind the first wave in the rip then "walking" the boat out and then back along the face of the rip. On some rips, the hot spot is the area where the rip bulges outward. Sometimes bass lay at the top of the bulge while other times they are on the edge of a rip bulge.

Bluefish tries for seconds, you've got his or her number. The stinger hook has the added benefit in this day of catch and release, of allowing an angler to set the hook sooner when a bass grabs the bait. You only have to let the fish have a count or one or two before setting up. More than likely you'll catch the fish in the corner of its jaw or just inside its mouth, places where the hook can be extracted with the least damage.

Prime locations to troll baits with wire are around offshore humps where bass hang out during the day. Among the best areas for wire line are rips. The astute wire troller puts out enough wire to get his or her bunker down near the bottom then positions the boat so the bait is just behind the curl of the rip's first wave as it's there the bass lie in hiding. With this accomplished, the helmsperson slowly trolls up and back along the face of the rip, all the while showing the lively, frisky bait to all creatures in residence.

Some rips might be only slight bulges on the water's surface that become apparent only with a stronger than normal tide on an ultra-flat day. Others are roaring, frothing lines of white that seem to go on forever. The former might only harbor a slight bump that's home to a few bass now and then. The other has more possibilities, but where along that line of curling water will the bass be found? One area that stands out more than others in the area from the rip at Bartlett's Reef off eastern Connecticut to the Old Man Rip south of Nantucket is a bulge. Find a location where the rip bulges out into the tide, then fish the apex of the bulge or on either side of it where it bends back into the main rip.

Don't be afraid to come back to a rip that's unproductive on the morning tide when she swings in the afternoon to flow from another direction. The ebb or dropping tide is usually superior but that generality goes out the window more

When trolling live bait, you must keep your thumb on the spool to prevent a backlash when a bass grabs the bait.

Bluefish, though acrobatic, are a secondary target for live bait trollers.

times than your sure bet in the football pool. And, don;t be afraid to troll around the hump or ridge that produces the rip during periods of slack tide. In certain areas you might be able to troll parallel to the hot spot rather than stemming to it at a right angle when the tide is humming.

While the big, frothing rip may grab the headlines in the fishing columns, there are hundreds of little rips that make up over smaller bumps that shouldn't be overlooked. Some of these small rockpiles, sometimes close to high traffic areas, yield bass when the time is right. If you're the sneaky type fisherman, you might wait until the fleet clears the inlet in the morning, then troll your bunker over the hump only one-eighth of a mile from the blinker atop the north jetty. Sometimes a potential wire line live bait hot spot will show up on your machine as a small mound, something that at first glance doesn't merit five minutes of time but, possibly in the quiet of a morning or evening, will house bass scrounging around the mussel-encrusted bottom for chow.

Other spots worth looking at are those old pilings that cause a tide boil in a tidal estuary. Perhaps you can troll your bait near those to catch the fish lurking downtide from them. The deeper edge of a sandbar up in a large bay or river might provide the same hunting grounds. Any place a current is interrupted has potential for you to troll your live bait. Usually the lazy creatures (most stripers are) will be positioned somewhere down current from the current break. In that way, they can watch what the tide brings them without expending much energy.

If you can troll a bunker spoon over the wreck of the F/V *No Hope*, as we stated earlier, you can most assuredly troll a live bunker. The bait has the added attraction of being able to swim on its own, so you can stop the boat a bit when the bait is right atop the money hole. Don't stop too long or you'll snag bottom, but the extra look is worth extra hits.

Another potential area for wire lining live bait is right around the bait itself. If bunkers are scattered over a wide area of ocean front, try trolling your baits down below the main schools. In that position they will be likely targets of opportunity for bass waiting to pick off stragglers from below. If a bass is watching 10 to 20 feet below the school, you bait may enter its field of vision right in front of its mouth.

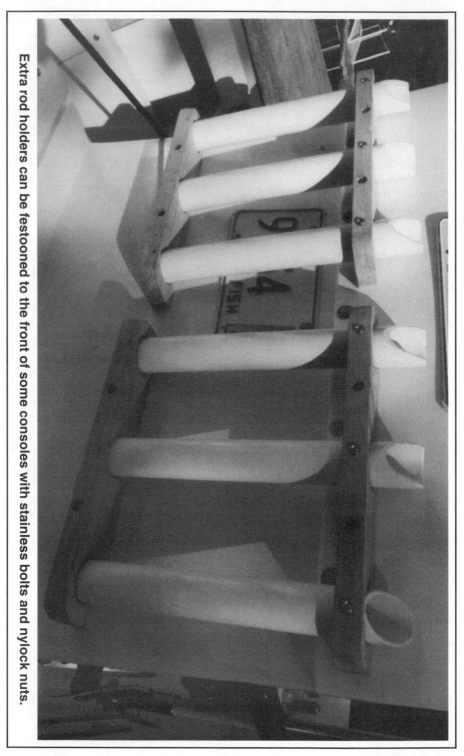

Extra rod holders can be festooned to the front of some consoles with stainless bolts and nylock nuts.

CHAPTER 19

Center Console Suggestions

Make Your Rig a Better Fishing Platform

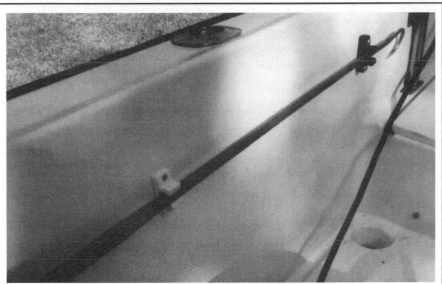

Small rubber holders keep a gaff at the ready.

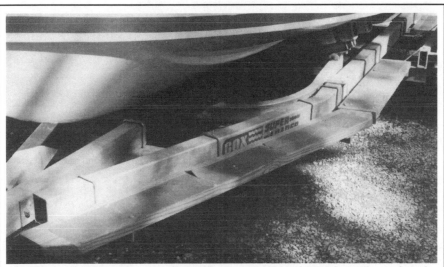

Custom walkboard on trailer allows one-man launch and retrieval.

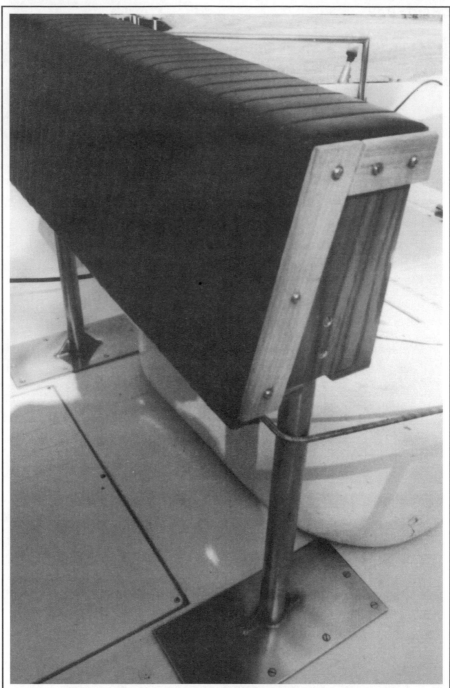

A custom leaning post can be constructed of Schedule 50, two-inch stainless pipe welded to a one-quarter inch plate bolted to the deck. Top is marine plywood coated with formica.

Forty-eight gallon bait tank is held in place behind the custom leaning post with a long bungee cord.

These trailer lights are portable, the bracket comes off with ease. Wire runs from starboard light to jack in rear bumper of the tow vehicle.

CAMP TR.
2805·82
CONNECTICUT

Some consoles can be built up to accept more electronics or provide more storage. This job was accomplished with one-half inch marine plywood that's been fiberglassed then painted with polyurethane paint.

This custom hand rail runs from mid-point of the console back to the stern. It's constructed of 1-1/4 inch stainless tubing welded together and screwed to the inside and bottom of the boat.

Lengthwise view of the author's old tin boat. It was a 14-footer that saw a lot of service.

CHAPTER 20

Tin Boat Tips

How to Set Up a 14' Fishing Machine

A hard wood floor (coated with Cuprinol) was installed between the middle and front seats. This can act as a platform for a large cooler used as a fish box, dry storage or bait tank.

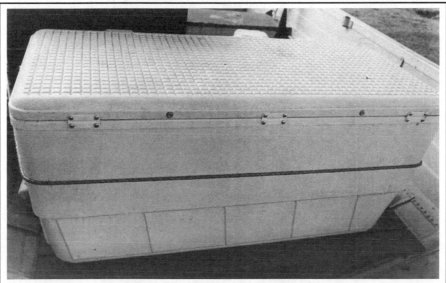

Large cooler in place on the flooring. Cooler is held there by a long bungee cord.

This small console, built on the middle seat, houses a paper machine and loran. Loran antenna is at right and folds down when not in use.

and 100 feet of rope on the other. A piece of wood shaped to the inside of the bow's vee holds the cleat.

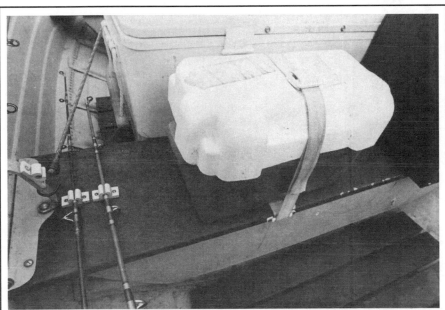

Spare battery strapped in atop the middle seat was used to run a pump when the cooler was used as a bait tank.

Extension handle allows the operator to stand while running the boat for maximum visibility.

Hardwood flooring between the middle and rear seats provides a level platform to ease the strain of a long fishing trip. The platform can be slipped out for cleaning or repair.

Tackle locker built atop rear seat takes up about three-quarters of the seat and is sturdy enough to sit on once the top is closed.

Flooring was also installed between the stern seat and the stern. The battery is strapped in place while wood blocks on top of the floor hold two six-gallon gas cans in place.

Rubber utility holders keep rods in place and secure.

If you're thinking about a wind dodger for your center console, you might consider one that folds down if you must clear a low bridge at high tide.

CHAPTER 21

Add-Ons and Additions

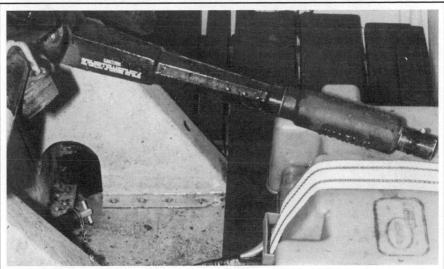

A lock bar on your small outboard keeps all the honest people honest. Just make sure you don't lose the key.

The forward console seat on this 23-footer was cut away allowing for more room for, in this case, a large bait cooler with cutting board glued on top.

If your older console boat has a rear seat that serves as a fish box, you can put fish in it without removing the top of the seat. Just cut out a section and hinge it. This type work might be best left to someone at a boatyard.

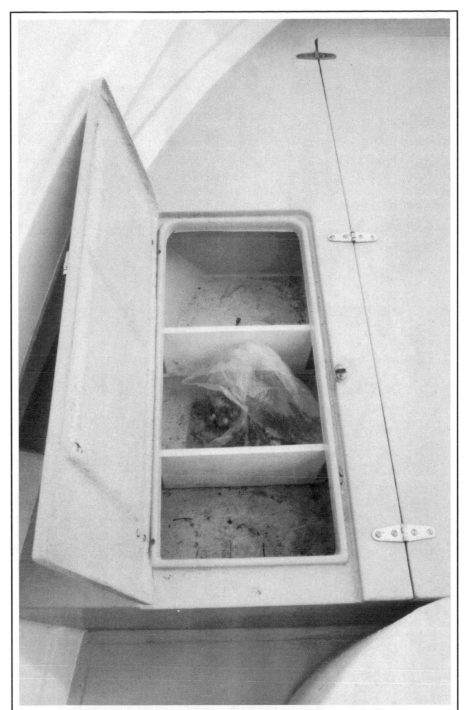

Forward compartments of this older model were compartmental-
ized to keep tackle separated.

Gaff made from a hockey stick will not roll off a gunnel.

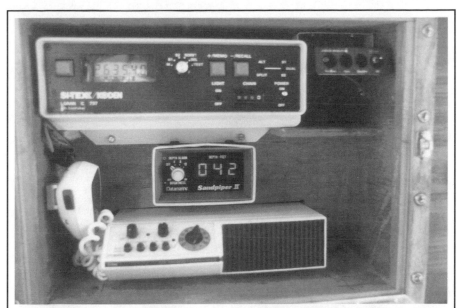

Woodwork by a boatyard puts electronics compactly inside a console.

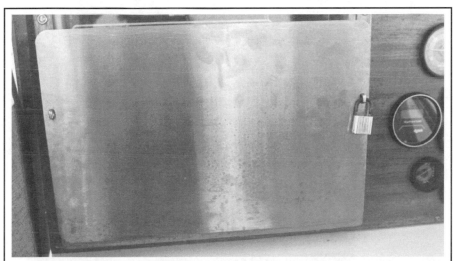

To keep the honest people from eying all your electronics when you're away from the boat, you can get a piece of metal fashioned to clip over the console front. A small lock further deters amateur thieves. This is ideal if you are traveling and spending the night away from your rig.

The present 30 pound test record for striped bass is the 71-pounder caught by John Baldino, on the right.

CHAPTER 22

Bass Records

Reprinted courtesy of IGFA

Bass, striped / *Morone saxatilis*

LINE CLASS	WEIGHT	PLACE	DATE	ANGLER
M-1 kg (2 lb)	9.53 kg (21 lb)	San Francisco Bay, California, USA	Jan. 20, 1992	Kirk E. Campbell
M-2 kg (4 lb)	18.37 kg (40 lb 8 oz)	Cape Cod Bay, Massachusetts, USA	May 25, 1985	Christopher Van Duzer
M-3 kg (6 lb)	25.79 kg (56 lb 14 oz)	Gay Head, Massachusetts, USA	Oct. 15, 1981	Richard C. Landon
M-4 kg (8 lb)	18.82 kg (41 lb 8 oz)	Fisher's Island, New York, USA	Aug. 27, 1995	Alan Golinski
M-6 kg (12 lb)	30.27 kg (66 lb 12 oz)	Bradley Beach, New Jersey, USA	Nov. 1, 1979	Steven R. Thomas
M-8 kg (16 lb)	31.29 kg (69 lb)	Sandy Hook, New Jersey, USA	Nov. 18, 1982	Thomas James Russell
M-10 kg (20 lb)	35.60 kg (78 lb 8 oz)	Atlantic City, New Jersey, USA	Sept. 21, 1982	Albert R. McReynolds
M-15 kg (30 lb)	32.20 kg (71 lb)	Norwalk, Connecticut, USA	July 14, 1980	John Baldino
M-24 kg (50 lb)	34.47 kg (76 lb)	Montauk, Long Island, New York, USA	July 17, 1981	Robert A. Rocchetta
M-37 kg (80 lb)	31.75 kg (70 lb)	Orient Point, New York, USA	Sept. 5, 1987	Chester A. Berry
W-1 kg (2 lb)	4.36 kg (9 lb 10 oz)	Cape Cod Bay, Massachusetts, USA	June 7, 1986	Sharyn Guggino
W-2 kg (4 lb)	13.77 kg (30 lb 6 oz)	Cape Cod Bay, Massachusetts, USA	May 24, 1985	Sharyn Guggino
W-3 kg (6 lb)	21.20 kg (46 lb 12 oz)	Fisher's Island, New York, USA	Sept. 4, 1995	Emme Golinski
W-4 kg (8 lb)	18.20 kg (40 lb 2 oz)	Millicoma River, Oregon, USA	April 5, 1985	Edna Skinner
W-6 kg (12 lb)	22.02 kg (48 lb 9 oz)	Deal, New Jersey, USA	July 27, 1980	Edna Yates
W-8 kg (16 lb)	21.99 kg (48 lb 8 oz)	Monomoy Island, Cape Cod, Mass., USA	July 16, 1991	Connie Codner
W-10 kg (20 lb)	26.08 kg (57 lb 8 oz)	Block Island Sound, New York, USA	Aug. 28, 1959	Mary R. Aubry
W-15 kg (30 lb)	29.25 kg (64 lb 8 oz)	North Truro, Massachusetts, USA	Aug. 14, 1960	Rosa O. Webb
W-24 kg (50 lb)	29.03 kg (64 lb)	Sea Bright, New Jersey, USA	June 27, 1971	Mrs. Asic Espenak
W-37 kg (80 lb)	25.40 kg (56 lb)	Sandy Hook, New Jersey, USA	June 7, 1955	Mrs. H. J. Sarnoski
W-37 kg (80 lb) Tie	25.40 kg (56 lb)	Montauk, New York, USA	Sept. 10, 1989	April Lynde Rocchetta

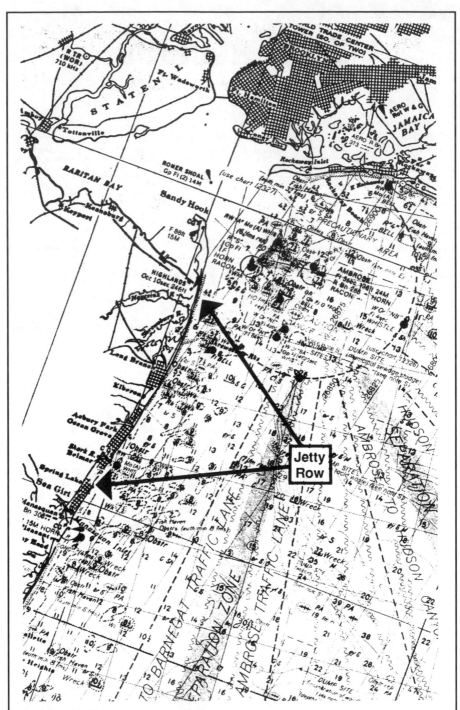

Jetty Row in northern New Jersey from Sandy Hook to Spring Lake is an ideal area to cast live eels into the front of the many jetties.

CHAPTER 23

Casting Eels

The night is black, quiet, without a sound of human involvement except your partner as he leans into another cast that sends a live eel shoreward in search of bass. Perhaps the eel hit in front of a jetty or perhaps a natural rock tossed by the late night sea. The angler might let the eel settle a bit or, then again, he or she might start a retrieve as soon as it hits the water. Fifteen feet from the start of the cast something nudges the eel, the lIne tIghtens and the angler comes back on the rod, driving the point hard into the jaw of a surprised striper. Another bass joins the ranks of 10 gadzillion or so fooled by cast eels over the last 40 years.

From Three Rock Pool on the south side of famed Cuttyhunk Island to the rocks of Jetty Row off northern New Jersey, anglers casting live eels account for bass from June through November. Some of the anglers catch their eels in the spring, keep them in live cars, then fish them after the herring runs of spring peter out.

To catch eels you can use the cylindrical, wire mesh, minnow traps for sale in most coastal bait stores. The traps can be baited with pieces of horseshoe crabs or mussels from the jetty's edge. Make sure you squash both baits

New England anglers have many rock areas into which to sling eels. Here Charley Soares is casting for fish off Newport, R. I.

Minnow trap with middle extension is an ideal live car to store eels under your boat at a marina.

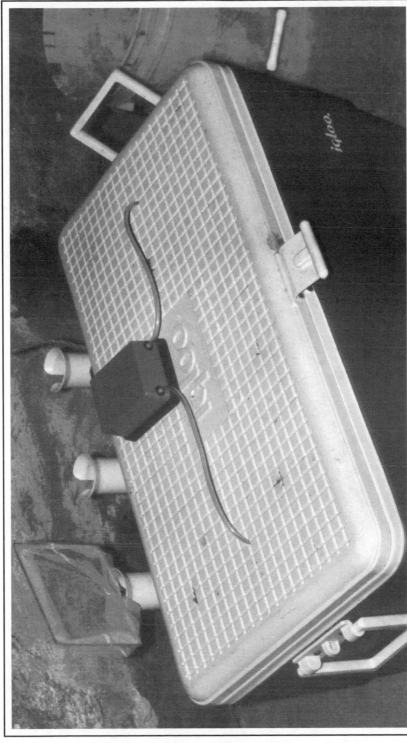

Eels can be stored at home, away from prying eyes, by mounting an aerator atop a small cooler. As long as the water is changed regularly and the cooler kept in a shady spot, your baits should last until your next fishing trip.

Tin boats are ideal machines to motor in close at night to sling eels. Just watch out for rocks and oncoming seas. This fish was caught off Fishers Island off the coast of southeastern Connecticut.

underfoot to let the juices seep out before depositing them in the traps. The pots can be set along tidal creeks or rivers or up in freshwater lakes or under spillways. The line from the traps can be tied to bushes or plastic milk bottles with the tops screwed on, the latter acting as markers to retrieve later on. Eels are nocturnal creatures, so let your traps soak during the evening. During the time I fished in New Jersey, we would set pots in the Flume at 8th Avenue in Asbury Park during a low tide late in the afternoon. We would then come back early in the morning of the next day or the low water occurring the following afternoon to, hopefully, pick up our eels.

Of course, there's an easier way by simply going into your coastal bait shop and buying the eels you need. If you buy them in bulk they can be stored in the same minnow trap under your boat at your marina. If that's a problem because of prying eyes, eels can be stored in your cellar in a cooler with an aquarium pump mounted atop it. The pump aerates the water which, in turn, keeps the eels alive and happy. You will have to change the water but this takes only a minute after you get home from work.

Different anglers have different preferences as to length of eels. Generally, baits in the 12 to 16-inch range will catch most fish in your neighborhood. To tote those size eels to your boat, a five-gallon plastic bucket will do just fine.

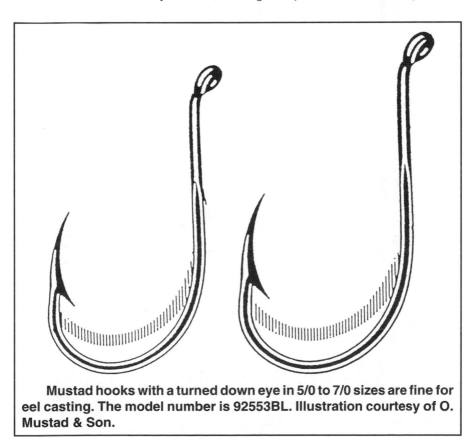

Mustad hooks with a turned down eye in 5/0 to 7/0 sizes are fine for eel casting. The model number is 92553BL. Illustration courtesy of O. Mustad & Son.

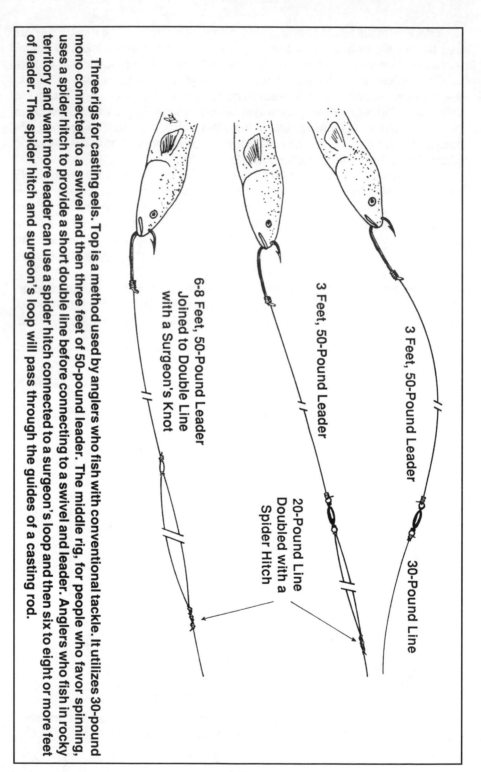

3 Feet, 50-Pound Leader

30-Pound Line

3 Feet, 50-Pound Leader

20-Pound Line
Doubled with a
Spider Hitch

6-8 Feet, 50-Pound Leader
Joined to Double Line
with a Surgeon's Knot

Three rigs for casting eels. Top is a method used by anglers who fish with conventional tackle. It utilizes 30-pound mono connected to a swivel and then three feet of 50-pound leader. The middle rig, for people who favor spinning, uses a spider hitch to provide a short double line before connecting to a swivel and leader. Anglers who fish in rocky territory and want more leader can use a spider hitch connected to a surgeon's loop and then six to eight or more feet of leader. The spider hitch and surgeon's loop will pass through the guides of a casting rod.

-142-

You'll also need a piece of rag to get a purchase on the slippery hide of an eel not thrilled that you've selected it to go find a bass.

Finding bass with eels means you and your boat are in tight to the structure. Ideal craft for that job are small, 14 or 16-foot, tin boats. These little craft draw little water and can get in tight with a minimum of noise or disturbance. A few tin boat anglers have electric motors mounted on the stern for the purpose of getting in on a Stealth mode.

Whatever craft is used, make sure of the location of rocks and other nasty stuff that eat lower units. A trip or two in daylight is mandatory when targeting new rockpiles for night casting. Also a must is an eye on oncoming seas. Don't get so engrossed in the fishing that you miss the comber that tips you over. A lost lower unit or capsizing could ruin your whole night.

Tackle for casting eels can be the same as described in the section on plugs. A spinning rod with 20 pound line, capable of tossing Danny plugs, will do for eels. Some anglers favor conventional tackle for this fishing, especially if bass hang out in rough areas. Some nights the only thing that saved a fish was that the 30-pound mono used by some conventional casters stood up to the abuse of being wrapped around some rocks before it came free. However, because of the ease of casting a wind resistant, live eel, spinning often is the preferred tackle.

The standard line for eel casting with spin gear is 20-pound test. If you're casting along a sandy stretch, 14 to 17-pound line might be fine, but the average fisherman who tosses eels into the fronts of man-made jetties or along boulder shores will probably do better with 20.

To rig up for eel casting, the conventional guys or gals might just tie a

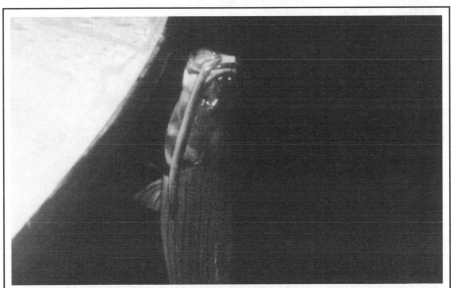

The single hook of eel casting makes it easy to release most of your fish to fight again.

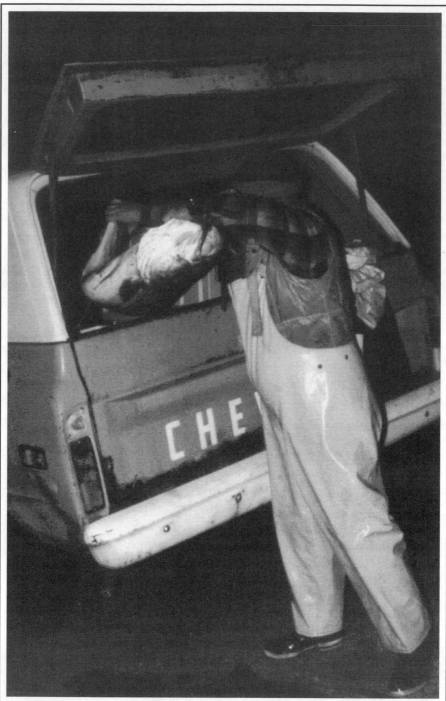

The end of a long night of casting; a trophy is loaded into the back of a truck at 3 a.m. for the trip home.

5/0 to 7/0 hook right to their 30-pound and start slinging. The spinners might use a small section of double line ahead of a three-foot piece of 50-pound leader. A Spider Hitch is fine for making the double line which is connected to a small, two-way swivel, in turn tied to the leader. If the spincaster fishes extremely tough ground, he or she can use more leader by tying the same Spider Hitch for double line but then connect that to a six to eight-foot section of 50-pound test with a surgeon's loop. The longer section of 50 may hold up as a large bass makes her way this way or that amongst the sunken stones.

Many hooks will do for live eel casting but one worth trying is the 92553BL from Mustad. It features a turned down eye for more direct pull to the line when you set the hook. It comes in a black finish and has the newer Accu Point sharpness Mustad is putting on some of their models. Sizes 5/0 to 7/0 should accommodate the bass eels the majority of fishermen like to use. The piece of rag brought along now lets you grasp the eel to run the hook point through the bottom jaw and out the top of the head.

After making the cast, some anglers immediately start a very slow retrieve while others may let the eel sink a bit. The hits are usually a tap followed by the line tightening. A rod's length of slack will allow a large bass to get the eel in position in its mouth. On other tides, the line will tighten fast then move away after a bass zeroed in swiftly for the kill. The hit from a bass will be steady while those from bluefish will be chopping, slashing strikes that reduce the eel to a cigar butt of head and neck. If the blues are too thick, you must find new casting grounds or fish your way through them in hopes a bass makes first contact on the next cast.

If a bass hits the bait but you miss hooking him, then he refuses to strike again, you might get a second hit by coming back to the spot later in the tide or you might position the boat so the eel comes at the fish from a different direction. Another tactic is to raise and then lower the tip of the rod slowly while retrieving. This gives the eel an undulating action that adds to its effectiveness.

Bass expert and friend, Charley Soares, related how he and his partners caught fish casting eels at Cuttyhunk Island when the phosphorescence known as "fire" made night fishing difficult. The tiny organisms in the water that cause the "fire" are disturbed by the passage of the bait and line, giving off a green glow that will spook most fish. The line looks like a hawser for the *Queen Mary* and the eel a creature from Mars. During those trying periods in the summer and early fall, Charley fooled bass by tossing the eel out, then merely letting it stay in place, not moving it much at all. This works, provided you've selected a location with bass in residence.

With the single hook in the eel, it's easy to unhook the fish and let it swim away after it's been held upright and moved back and forth in the water to allow water to pass through its gills. The more bass released, the better chances for good fishing on your day off the same time next year and the year after and the year after ...

Small black tubes rigged on 3/16-inch tubing are deadly on um-brella rigs when bass are chasing sand eels.

CHAPTER 24

Umbrella Rig Basics

If umbrellas were food, some anglers would look on them as broccoli, a substance to be avoided at all costs. But, given a little time and practice, umbrella rigs can catch with the best of them. If you doubt this, just watch a seasoned charter skipper; in his or her hands the gawky, dangling rigs become a deadly tool.

There are dozens of rigs around, so a fair question from a would-be striper seeker is which ones have bettered the test of time and fish? For an answer to that we again sought the advice of Captain Kerry Douton of J&B Tackle in

Crimps at midpoint on umbrella rig arms keep the teaser from fouling by flipping back over the arm and keep them in place.

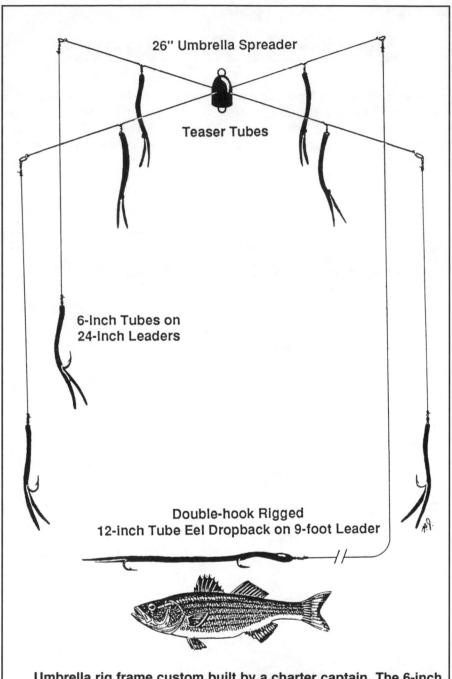

26" Umbrella Spreader

Teaser Tubes

6-inch Tubes on
24-Inch Leaders

Double-hook Rigged
12-inch Tube Eel Dropback on 9-foot Leader

Umbrella rig frame custom built by a charter captain. The 6-inch tubes are strung back from the outside arms with 24-inch pieces of leader material. The long dropback to a two-hook tube from one of the outside arms is a killer for large bass.

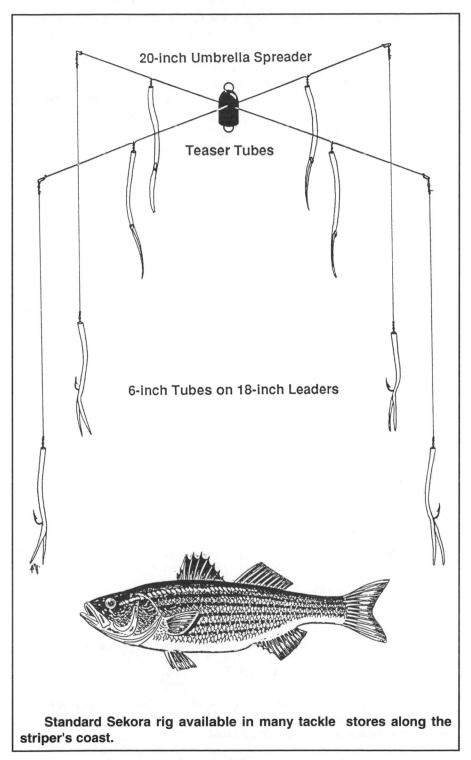

20-inch Umbrella Spreader

Teaser Tubes

6-inch Tubes on 18-inch Leaders

Standard Sekora rig available in many tackle stores along the striper's coast.

Niantic, Connecticut. Kerry has been in the tackle business for 20 years and, among his many customers, are some of the best charter skippers on the coast. Kerry has seen what's selling; what's catching.

For fishermen looking to buy a rig right off the shelf, Kerry recommends the #40R-225 by Sekora Tackle in Montauk, N.Y. These rigs are available up and down the coast, big stores or small. An angler can take one out of the pack, clip it to the snap swivel of his wire line rig, and begin fishing.

The arms on the Sekora rig measure 20 inches across each of the two arms that are set 90 degrees to each other through a lead centerpiece, the classic profile of the umbrella rig. At the end of each arm is a 1/0 swivel attached to a 14-inch piece of heavy mono in turn attached to a #40, six-inch Sekora tube. Best colors over the years have been white, black, red and an olive green. Those four hues fooled more bass than all other colors of the spectrum.

Midway down the arms from the lead center weight are a couple of small metal sleeves held in place by a small bend in the wire. In between the sleeves

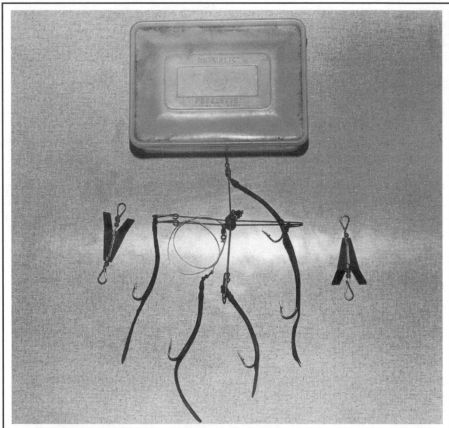

Some anglers favor small, compact rigs such as this one manufactured by Zing Products in Fall River, Mass. The addition of spinners between tubes and the rig's arms adds flash.

is a surge tube the same size as the ones on the outside of the arms, only those carry no hooks. These are there only as teasers or attractors. The idea of the umbrella is to represent a school of fish to a lurking striper. The teasers help "flesh" out the rig to give the appearance of a group of forage fish swimming up against the tide. In addition to the four tubes with hooks and the four teasers, there's space under the lead centerpiece to attach a longer leader, say four to six feet, then attach a large lure like a swimming plug or larger tube. The idea behind this move is to simulate a larger fish chasing a school of bait. Big bass or blues will zero in on the larger bait thinking it a better meal.

While Sekora rigs are fine, charter skippers up and down the coast make their own because of cost or other factors. One such person is Captain Joe Wysocki of the *Osprey*. He makes four-arm rigs that measure 26 inches across, making them that much harder to tangle. Kerry said he usually completes Joe's creations by adding three #40 Sekora tubes to the outside of the arms. He adds them by using a 24-inch piece of 60 to 80-pound Perlon, which is stiff leader material. Kerry feels strongly the stiffer leader material keeps the tubes from tangling much, this increasing chances the tubes will be "swimming." A tube on an umbrella doesn't actually swim side to side like a plug. Rather, it spins around an axis, giving the impression of swimming motion. On the fourth arm of the larger rig, Kerry attaches a nine-foot piece of Perlon and on this he rigs a #62 Sekora tube. These tubes measure 12 inches long and carry one hook in their midpoint, one in their tail end. The idea behind this bigger trailer is the same as a swimming plug. A bass will usually pick out the larger prey thinking it the better target.

Like the Sekora rigs, the custom version also features metal sleeves attached to the midpoint of the four arms. The teaser tubes, rigged with bead chain or swivels, are attached around the umbrella arm between those sleeves. This arrangement prevents the teaser from flipping back around the arm of the rig and taking it out of action. Teasers need not swim as well as the outside tubes for the rig to work. They are there mainly to add bulk, to give the impression of more baitfish to a bass.

Kerry doesn't recommend mixing colors on rigs. If he has all red tubes and teasers, he'll put a red trailer tube off the odd arm. He is secure in his feeling the trailer rigged off an outside arm catches better than one down the center. And, he has a lot of pictures of 40 to 50-pound bass caught by his charter captain customers to prove his point.

To fish umbrella rigs, use the wire line rod listed in the earlier chapter on wire basics. Attach a 15 to 20-foot leader to the wire, then a sturdy snap swivel to it. Clip the swivel onto the eye of the center weight, then carefully place it overboard. You don't want to throw an umbrella over the side then quickly let out line. More than likely the rig will tangle and you might snag bottom. Instead, hold the leader in your hand, then place the rig in the water by the side of the boat. After making sure the outside tubes are spinning and the trailer working, gradually let out line by stripping an arm's length at a time from the reel. With your other hand, keep your thumb on the spool to prevent overrun. When enough of the line begins to move out by itself, keep pressure on the spool to assure the rig will sink without tangling and will not strike the bottom. If it does, reel it back immediately and check for weed or debris. A fouled rig will not catch.

Most umbrella fishing is done around rips or the high points or edges of structures. The average bass angler will probably have 300 feet of wire on the reel so that means he or she can work down to about 40 feet, depending on time and tide.

Practice, practice, and more hard work will earn you a gold star in umbrella management. If there's a charter boat nearby, don't get in its way, but try to notice what he's doing that you're not. Perhaps he's on a range that's only a one or two boat spot and your rig is the odd vessel out. Perhaps he has his trailer rigged in a different fashion or maybe he's whackin' em with black while you've got on your favorite olive green.

A couple of the don'ts of umbrella fishing are: don't make sharp turns and don't turn downtide. You will foul the rig, hang bottom or tangle the boat next door if you're fishing gunnel to gunnel, stemming up from a small spot. Instead, make shallow turns and always work up against the flow.

Get in the habit of thinking of where the rig is, not where you are. Remember, the rig might be 30-plus feet down, 300 feet away from you. If your boat is right atop the proper ranges that means your rig isn't. If the boat is uptide of the structure, you have a chance. Try this some afternoon when fishing is stinko. Drop a marker buoy, then practice putting your umbrella near the spot with enough wire to keep it within six feet of the bottom. If you're grabbing bottom, shorten the wire. If you're catching on the strength of the tide, you may also have to shorten the wire again as the tide eases off. If the wind becomes stronger as the tide slacks, you may have to adjust your next trolling pass accordingly. Remember to think in terms of the location of the rig, not your steering wheel.

Since most wire rods have gimbals on their butts, anglers usually place the rods in their flush mount holders, then practice the craft of putting the rig on home base. Some anglers, however, keep the rod in their hands, then slowly bring the rig forward a bit, then drop it back. The surging ahead a little faster than the boat, then easing backwards (all the while keeping a tight line) sometimes works wildly well. On other days it gives the purchase of this book a little exercise while the dead stick rod catches as well or better.

If the leaders to your tubes become chafed, change them at first opportunity. It might pay to have some leaders tied up beforehand so ,when one looks doubtful, you just unclip it and substitute one at the ready. If you're not getting any action and conditions look good, try changing colors or check for weeds or a tangled rig. Don't ride around the ocean all morning without a systems check every now and then.

If you're out for bass at the never-fail honey bucket and are "lucky" enough to load the rig with jumbogator bluefish, you can forego trial by teeth by merely unhooking the rig, then dropping the snapping mass in the fishbox until everyone quiets down. Having another rig at the ready completes this procedure. If you don't want the blues, by all means take the time to unhook them so they live another day.

While most of the pros we've spoken to felt the longer arm rigs were the best, there's a mini-version of an umbrella rig that some private boaters do favor. Manufactured by Zing products in Fall River, Massachusetts, these rigs measure 12 inches across their two arms. They may have a tendency to tangle more than their longer-arm cousins but this feature is minor when compared to their storage capabilities. Two or three of these small rigs can be stored in a plastic container which easily fits under the console of Mr. or Ms. average bass boat.

To rig these small rigs, anglers usually place tubes right in the snap on the outside of the arms. The small diameter of the rigs precludes dropping back the outside tubes on strands of leader because of tangling. Some fishermen like to add a bit of flash to the rigs, so they place heavy spinners between the tubes and the arms. Once the four tubes and/or spinners are in place, some fishermen simply place a fifth spinner/tube down from the center weight. Friend and proficient bassman Charley Soares once caught a 50-plus pounder on one of the small rigs rigged in just such a fashion. Charley figures the fish rushed what it saw as a compact school of sand eels, thus increasing its chances for a kill. This idea is borne out time and time again when bass fooled on the small rig have more than one tube in their mouths. If you don't like the idea of fishing all the tubes at the same distance, you can opt for a trailer going back from the bottom eye of the center weight as far as you desire. If you're unsure of how far to drop a trailer on the small rig, try two to four feet.

Another wrinkle used by fans of the mini-rigs is small diameter tubing, especially when sand eels are about. Instead of fishing tubing with 5/16 or 7/16-inch inside diameter (standard on most rigs), try black tubing with a 3/16-inch diameter. Rigged on a 5/0 Limerick with small swivel, these are dead ringers with a sand eel silhouette. Adjust the length of your tubes to the size of the baits. If you have trouble getting the tubing over a hook or swivel, try Lux Liquid. The tubing should then slide up in place without any more problems. For maximum action, some private boat anglers rig small tubes on short sections of bead chain rather than swivels, though corrosion-free swivels work fine. If you desire more action from the tubes, put a steeper bend in the hook.

If you're new to bassin', we'd recommend studying the pros: get larger rigs first, they don't tangle as much so they reduce the amount of Rolaids you'll need as you practice, practice, practice.

Master bass fisherman Sherwood Lincoln with a rod made for three waying with heavy sinkers in deep, swift currents.

CHAPTER 25

Some Bass Rods
DRIFT ROD
Three-Waying in Fast Deep Water

Lamiglass MB-1083M Blank
Fuji #22 FPS Reel Seat
14-inch Hypalon near grip
5-inch Hypalon fore grip
One inch butt cap
Guides are Fuji BNHG type

Blank Is cut back to a
#16 top

Guide sizes, tip to butt:

#16 - Top
#12 - First guide
#16 - Second guide
#16 - Third guide
#20 - Fourth guide
#20 - Fifth guide

Guide spacing:
Tip to center of first guide	6-1/2 inches
First to second guide	8 inches
Second to third guide	9-1/2 inches
Third to fourth guide	10-1/2 inches
Fourth to fifth guide	11 inches

CONVENTIONAL ROD
Casting Live Eels

Lamiglas BT963M blank
Fuji FPS20 reel seat
13-inch Hypalon butt grip
6-inch Hypalon fore grip
Fuji #22 gimbal or butt cap
Guides are Fuji BNLG type

Blank is cut back 12
inches from the butt

Guide sizes, top to butt:

#8 BPLT tip
#8 - First guide
#8 - Second guide
#10 - Third guide
#10 - Fourth guide

#12 - Fifth guide
#16 - Sixth guide
#20 - Seventh guide

Guide spacing:

Tip to center of first guide	4 inches
First to second guide	5 inches
Second to third guide	5-3/4 inches
Third to fourth guide	5-7/8 inches
Fourth to fifth guide	7-1/4 inches
Fifth to sixth guide	8-1/4 inches
Sixth to seventh guide	9 inches

SPINNING ROD
Casting Live Eels and Plugs

Lamiglas BT963M blank
Fuji FPS 20 reel seat
13-inch Hypalon butt grip   Blank is cut back
6-inch Hypalon fore grip   9 inches from the tip
Fuji #22 gimbal or butt cap
Guides are Fuji BSVLGs, two-footed guides

Guide sizes, tip to butt: #12 BPLT top
                                   #12 - First guide
                                   #16 - Second guide
                                   #20 - Third guide
                                   #20 - Fourth guide
                                   #30 - Fifth guide
                                   #40 - Sixth guide

Guide spacing:

Tip to center of first guide	4 inches
First to second guide	5-1/4 inches
Second to third guide	6-1/2 inches
Third to fourth guide	7-3/4 inches
Fourth to fifth guide	9 inches
Fifth to sixth guide	10-1/2 inches

LIVE LINING ROD
Conventional Rod for Bunker Fishing

Lamiglas BT963M blank
Fuji FPS #20 reel seat
13-inch butt grip   Blank is cut back
6-inch fore grip   14 inches from the tip
Fuji #22 gimbal or butt cap
Guides are Fuji BNLG type

Guide sizes, tip to butt: #14 BPLT tip
                                      #12 - First guide
                                      #12 - Second guide
                                      #12 - Third guide
                                      #16 - Fourth guide
                                      #16 - Fifth guide
                                      #20 - Sixth guide

Guide spacing:
    Tip to center of first guide   5-1/2 inches
    First to second guide   5-1/2 inches
    Second to third guide   6-1/4 inches
    Third to fourth guide   7-1/4 inches
    Fourth to fifth guide   8-3/4 inches
    Fifth to sixth guide   11 inches

ULTRALIGHT SPIN ROD
Casting Small Plugs

Lamiglas GUL601 blank
Fuji FPS #16 reel seat
2-inch butt grip   Blank is left as is.
2-inch fore grip
Butt plug or butt cap
Guides are Fuji BLVLG type

Guide sizes, tip to butt: #5 BPLT tip
                                      #8 - First guide
                                      #10 - Second guide
                                      #16 - Third guide
                                      #20 - Fourth guide
                                      #25 - Fifth guide

Guide spacing:

Tip to center of first guide	4 inches
First to second guide	4-1/2 inches
Second to third guide	6 inches
Third to fourth guide	8 inches
Fourth to fifth guide	10 inches

LIGHT CASTING AND POPPING ROD

Shakespeare GC90-5   1D#95-97
Fuji T-20P reel seat
8-1/2-inch butt grip   Blank left as is
6-inch fore grip
2-inch butt cap
Guides are Fuji BNL6 type

Guides: #6 Fuji tip
                                          Smaller sized guides, but these
        might vary due to individual

                                          taste and requirements

Guide spacing:

Tip to center of first guide	4 inches
First to second guide	4-1/2 inches
Second to third guide	4-3/4 inches
Third to fourth guide	5 inches
Fourth to fifth guide	5-3/4 inches
Fifth to sixth guide	7 inches
Sixth to seventh guide	8-3/8 inches
Seventh to eighth guide	10-3/4 inches
Eighth to reel seat center	29 inches

Captain Bill Herold with the light casting and popping rod made from a Shakespeare blank.

About the Author

Tim Coleman has fished from different beaches, rockpiles, private and charter boats since he was six. He's made a lot of life's decisions on the need to be near the water. His interest in angling was interrupted for service in Vietnam and, afterwards, a B. A. degree in journalism from the University of Rhode Island.

The love of fishing led him to his present job as Managing Editor of *The New England Fisherman* and Senior Editor of The Fisherman Group. Over the 23 years he's worked for the magazine, he's written over 1,000 articles and columns. His freelance credits include *Outdoor Life, Saltwater Sportsman, Garcia Fishing Annual, Pennsylvania Angler*, Mercury Marine's *Outdoors* and *Florida Fishing News*. Besides magazine articles, Coleman is the author of *Bass From the Beach, Codfishing in New England, Offshore Fishing* and *Fishing Connecticut Waters* and co-author of *The First Book of Angling Ideas* and *Fishable Wrecks and Rockpiles.*